First World War
and Army of Occupation
War Diary
France, Belgium and Germany

24 DIVISION
Divisional Troops
191 Machine Gun Company
13 December 1916 - 28 February 1918

WO95/2201/3

The Naval & Military Press Ltd
www.nmarchive.com
Published in association with The National Archives

Published by

The Naval & Military Press Ltd

Unit 10 Ridgewood Industrial Park,

Uckfield, East Sussex,

TN22 5QE England

Tel: +44 (0) 1825 749494

www.naval-military-press.com

www.nmarchive.com

This diary has been reprinted in facsimile from the original. Any imperfections are inevitably reproduced and the quality may fall short of modern type and cartographic standards.

© Crown Copyright
Images reproduced by permission of The National Archives, London, England, 2015.

Contents

Document type	Place/Title	Date From	Date To
Heading	WO95/2201-3		
Heading	191st Machine Gun Coy. Dec 1916 1916 Feb		
War Diary	In The Field	13/12/1916	31/03/1917
Heading	191st Machine Gun Company 24th Division April 1917		
War Diary	In the Field	01/04/1917	31/05/1917
Miscellaneous	24th Division No. M. 132	17/07/1917	17/07/1917
War Diary	In the Field	01/06/1917	31/08/1917
Heading	191 M.G. Coy Vol 10		
War Diary	In the Field	01/09/1917	30/09/1917
Heading	War Diary of 191 M.G. Coy For October 1917		
War Diary	Hesbecourt & Line	01/10/1917	10/10/1917
War Diary	Roisel & Line	11/10/1917	31/10/1917
War Diary	War Diary 191st Machine Gun Company. From Nov 1st to Nov 30th 1917		
War Diary	Roisel	01/11/1917	26/02/1918
War Diary	Berteaucourt	27/02/1918	28/02/1918

woas/2201/3

24TH DIVISION
DIVL TROOPS

191ST MACHINE GUN COY.
DEC 1916 - ~~MAY 1919~~
1918 FEB

24TH DIVISION
DIVL TROOPS

Army Form C. 2118.

WAR DIARY
INTELLIGENCE SUMMARY
(Erase heading not required.)

Place	Date	Hour	Summary of Events and Information	Remarks and references to Appendices
In the Field	13/12/16	11.0 a.m.	Arrived Havre. Bus. embarked all correct.	
"		6.30 p.m.	Arrived No 1 Rest Camp Havre. Rained all day.	
In the Field	14/12/16	9.0 a.m.	Medical Inspection of Company. One man ordered to hospital with Scabies.	
"		5.0 p.m.	Left Rest Camp Havre. Proceeded to station for entraining.	
"		9.0 p.m.	Entraining complete. Rained all day.	
In the Field	15/12/16	12.20 p.m.	Arrived Abbeville. 5 hours late according to "Ordre de transport". Half an hour allowed for watering animals & making tea for men. Weather fine.	
"		12.55 p.m.	Left Abbeville.	
"		7.45 p.m.	Arrived Bethune. Raining.	
"		8.0 p.m.	Received movement order to proceed to Noeux les Mines	
"		8.10 p.m.	Train left Bethune	
"		9.0 p.m.	Arrived Noeux les Mines. Detrained & marched men to billets & animals to stable. Raining.	

Army Form C. 2118.

WAR DIARY
or
INTELLIGENCE SUMMARY
(Erase heading not required.)

Place	Date	Hour	Summary of Events and Information	Remarks and references to Appendices
In the Field	16/12/16	9.0 am	Reported to Town Major Nreux les Mines. Drew rations for 16th & 17th inst. Issued Steel Helmets, Leather jerkins &c to Company. Unpacked stores. Cleaned guns. Fine day.	
In the Field	17/12/16	9.0 am 12.30 pm 4.0 pm	Church Parades. (Fine day)	
In the Field	18/12/16	9.0 am 2.0 pm	Washing limbers. Cleaning Harness & general routine work. Drew box respirators. Issued same to men. Men went through gas chamber. (Fine day).	
In the Field	19/12/16	9.0 am 10.0 am	Company inspected by G.O.C. 24th Division. Preparation for moving to Les Brebis. (Fine day)	

Army Form C. 2118.

WAR DIARY
or
INTELLIGENCE SUMMARY

(Erase heading not required.)

Place	Date	Hour	Summary of Events and Information	Remarks and references to Appendices
In the Field	20/12/16	9.0 am	Fine frosty morning. Left Noeux les Mines for les Brebis. Company marched past General Capper. Transport not satisfactory to G.O.C. Warned Transport officer that transport must be greatly improved in less than a week or would have to move.	
		10.30	Arrived les Brebis. Billetted troops & animals. Reported to 73rd Brigade 12 noon.	
		2.0 pm	Reported to 17th Brigade.	
		3.0 pm	Visited Brigade M.G.O. 17th Brigade.	
		4.0 pm	Visited Brigade M.G.O. 73rd Brigade.	
		6.0 pm	Reported at 73 Inf Brigade for interview with Brig. General. He was not in.	
		9.30 pm	Reported again at 73 Inf Brigade, & interviewed Brig. General.	

WAR DIARY or INTELLIGENCE SUMMARY

Army Form C. 2118.

Place	Date	Hour	Summary of Events and Information	Remarks and references to Appendices
In the Field	21/12/16	10.0 am.	Visited Brigade M.G.O 17th Inf Brigade & arranged for instruction in trenches of 2 sections of my Company.	
		11.0 am.	Interviewed Corps M.G.O.	
		2.0 pm.	Interviewed Staff Capt. 73rd Inf. Brigade re unsatisfactory stabling.	
		2.30 pm.	Interviewed Town Major Le Bretro re stabling.	
			Company washed limbers, cleaned harness. Gas helmet drill &c. Fine day.	
In the Field	22/12/16	9.0 am	2nd Lts Colliver, Jones & James inspected trenches of 17th Inf. Brigade	
			Company Gas helmet drill. Cleaning guns, limbers & harness. Raining in morning. Fine in afternoon.	
In the Field	23/12/16	9.0 am	Routine work.	
		1.0 pm	No 1 Section left for a weeks instruction in trenches with 73 Inf M.G.Coy.	
		2.0 pm	Visit Town Major re transport hire. Windy & raining	

Army Form C. 2118.

WAR DIARY
INTELLIGENCE SUMMARY
(Erase heading not required.)

Instructions regarding War Diaries and Intelligence Summaries are contained in F. S. Regs., Part II. and the Staff Manual respectively. Title Pages will be prepared in manuscript.

Place	Date	Hour	Summary of Events and Information	Remarks and references to Appendices
In the Field	24/12/16		Fine day.	
		12.0(noon)	Church Parade.	
		11.30	Inspection of Transport by O/C Divisional Train. Great improvement in Transport. 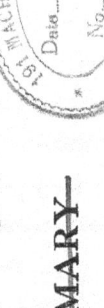	
In the Field	25/12/16		Xmas day. Fine day.	
In the Field	26/12/16	9.0 am	Routine work including gas helmet drill.	
		11.0 am	Visited trenches emplacements etc of 73 M.G. Coy with other O.'s in Command). Fine in morning, rained in afternoon.	
In the Field	27/12/16	9.0 am	Routine work by Company. Received orders to move to Mory in, gate. Visited Town Major Mory infants re billets. Fine day.	

Army Form C. 2118.

Instructions regarding War Diaries and Intelligence Summaries are contained in F. S. Regs., Part II. and the Staff Manual respectively. Title Pages will be prepared in manuscript.

WAR DIARY
or
INTELLIGENCE SUMMARY
(Erase heading not required.)

Place	Date	Hour	Summary of Events and Information	Remarks and references to Appendices
In the Field	28/12/16	9.0	Company move to-day up a der.	
		9.0	Received orders to move to Loos. Visited Loos & interviewed Commandant & O/C Motor Machine Gun Batt. Fine day.	
In the Field	29/12/16	10.0 am	Company moved to Loos by sections at hrly intervals. Took over gun positions allotted to me by Commandant Loos Defences. Reported all complete at 6.0 pm. Very well.	
In the Field	30/12/16		Weather unsettled. Inspected gun positions. Practice gas alarm at 5.0 pm. at which all teams stood to. Teams rested during the day. Attitude of Hun very quiet.	

Army Form C. 2118.

WAR DIARY
or
INTELLIGENCE SUMMARY
(Erase heading not required.)

Place	Date	Hour	Summary of Events and Information	Remarks and references to Appendices
In the Field	31/12/16		Teams at work on falls & dug outs. Weather unsettled. Six guns to fire at intervals during the night.	

C. J. Cross Capt.
Commanding 191 M.G. Coy.

Army Form C. 2118.

WAR DIARY
or
INTELLIGENCE SUMMARY

191 M.A. Coy

Vol 2

(Erase heading not required.)

Instructions regarding War Diaries and Intelligence Summaries are contained in F. S. Regs., Part II. and the Staff Manual respectively. Title Pages will be prepared in manuscript.

Place	Date	Hour	Summary of Events and Information	Remarks and references to Appendices
In the Field	1/1/1917	12 MID NT.	Inspected guns. Commenced work on new dug outs. Fired on German back areas. Weather Fine.	
In the Field	2/1/1917	4:30 am	Inspected guns. Men working on emplacements, cleaning trenches. Fired on German back areas & ration dumps. Weather Fine.	
In the Field	3/1/1917	12:15 am 9.0 12.0 M/D N/GHT	Fired on German ration dumps. Inspected guns. Men working on gun emplacement & cleaning trenches. German Artillery active. Fired machine fire on back areas of German lines. Weather Fine.	
In the Field	4/1/1917		Visit des Brelles, interview at Brigade Office. Inspected trenches at May infanterie & limbers. Great improvement in cleanliness of trenches. Weather unsettled. Company working on new dug out no 49. Laying duck boards to emplacements.	

2449 Wt. W14957/M90 750,000 1/16 J.B.C. & A. Forms/C.2118/12.

Army Form C. 2118.

WAR DIARY
or
INTELLIGENCE SUMMARY
(Erase heading not required.)

191 M.G. Coy

Place	Date	Hour	Summary of Events and Information	Remarks and references to Appendices
In the Field	5/1/17		Weather Fine. Company working on new emplacements C Keep. Dug out A9, emplacement A6. No 1 Section relieves No 3 Section in C Keep.	
		10.0 pm	Indirect fire on German ration dumps.	
In the Field	6/1/17		Weather Fine. Repairing emplacements, dug outs & trenches	
In the Field	7/1/17		Weather Fine. Men working on No. A9. Dug out, A6 emplacement self filling. Repairing purposes D1 position	
		10.0 pm	Indirect fire on German back areas.	
In the Field	8/1/17		Weather Fine. Men working on B1a emplacement, repairing trenches. Received orders that the Company will be attached to 72nd Coy	
		4:30 to 6:30 am	Indirect fire on German ration dumps.	

Army Form C. 2118.

WAR DIARY
or
INTELLIGENCE SUMMARY

(Erase heading not required.)

191 M.G. Coy

Place	Date	Hour	Summary of Events and Information	Remarks and references to Appendices
In the Field	9/1/17		Weather fine. Visit Philosophe. Interview O/C 72 M.G. Coy. Visit House des Brynes. Interview 73rd Infy Brigade re Bribio. Inspects Transport Maynpale. Men on routine work.	
In the Field	10/1/17		Weather unsettled. No 3 Section takes over anti aircraft guns. House des Brynes. Men working in new dug out & repairs to trench.	
		9.0 pm to 4.0 am (11/1/17)	Fired on German ration dumps.	
In the Field	11/1/17		Visit House des Brynes, inspect gun emplacement. Visit Mazingarbe & inspect Transport & Quartermasters stores. Visit 17th Brigade Hqrs. Weather unsettled.	
		9.0 pm 3.0 am (12-1-17)	Fired on German Back area & ration dumps.	
In the Field	12/1/17		Weather unsettled. G.O.C. inspects gun emplacements. various matters to be remedied.	
		9.0 pm 12.0 pm	Indirect fire on German Back area & ration dumps.	

Army Form C. 2118.

WAR DIARY
or
INTELLIGENCE SUMMARY

(Erase heading not required.)

191 M-G. Coy

Instructions regarding War Diaries and Intelligence Summaries are contained in F.S. Regs., Part II. and the Staff Manual respectively. Title Pages will be prepared in manuscript.

Place	Date	Hour	Summary of Events and Information	Remarks and references to Appendices
In the field	13/1/17		Weather. Wet & snow. Men working on new emplacements for nights firing. Cleaning trenches.	
In the field	14/1/17	10.0 pm	Weather fine. Inspect proposed new emplacements A Key. Indirect fire on German rear areas.	
In the field	15/1/17	9.0 pm to 6.0 am (16/1/17)	Fine. Dull. Routine work. Indirect fire on German rations dumps & rear areas. Pte Lambs [?] accidentally wounded.	
In the field	16/1/17	9.0 pm to 6.0 am (17/1/17)	Weather unsettled. Visit 17th Brigade, Zonn Major de Bretia, Inspector Transport wagonate. Inspected guns at Nouvex les Mines. Company in training business, repairing trenches. Indirect fire on German ration dumps & rear areas.	

2449. Wt. W14957/M90 750,000 1/16 J.B.C. & A. Forms/C.2118/12.

WAR DIARY
or
INTELLIGENCE SUMMARY

(Erase heading not required.)

Army Form C. 2118.

1914 M.G. Coy

Place	Date	Hour	Summary of Events and Information	Remarks and references to Appendices
In the Field	17/1/17		Weather thawing. Visit of OC "D" Keep. Company wiring Crozier, making dug outs &c.	
		10.0 pm	Indirect fire in German ration dumps.	
In the Field	18/1/17		Weather snowing. Went round emplacements with Camouflage Officer. Men working on new emplacement A Keep. Inspected the new emplacement with Commander.	
		9.30 pm to 6.0 am (19/1/17)	Indirect fire on German rear areas, roads & ration dumps.	
In the Field	19/1/17		Weather fine. Visit Douve les Trois. Inspected gun emplacement. Company working on new emplacement A Keep.	
		10.30 pm to 12.40 PM Midnight	Dug into & cleaning trenches.	
			Indirect fire on German rear areas, ration dumps & roads.	
In the Field	20/1/17		Weather cold, fine, frosty. Visit C Keep with OC. Men working on new emplacement A Keep. Men dug out & cleaning trenches.	
		9.0 pm to 6.30 am (21/1/17)	Indirect fire in German back areas, & ration dumps.	

Army Form C. 2118.

WAR DIARY
or
INTELLIGENCE SUMMARY

(Erase heading not required.)

191st M.G. Coy

Place	Date	Hour	Summary of Events and Information	Remarks and references to Appendices
In the Field	21/1/17		Weather fine & frosty. Men working on new emplacement A Coy. Building new dug out. Indirect fire on German rear areas, return dumps & roads.	
		9.0 pm to 6.0 am (22/1/17)		
In the Field	22/1/17		Weather frosty. Men working on new emplacement A. Coy. New dug out. A Party detailed for Salvage work. Indirect fire on German rear areas & return dumps.	
		9.0 pm to 12.0 am (Midnight)		
In the Field	23/1/17		Weather fine, frosty. Visit Brig_ from adj_ interviewed 17th Inf Brigade. Visit O.C. 17 M.G. Coy re proposed raid on 26th inst. Agreed to supply 3 guns to assist. Inspected transport. Company in new emplacement. A Coy. & general routine work.	

Army Form C. 2118.

WAR DIARY
or
INTELLIGENCE SUMMARY

191M.G.Coy

(Erase heading not required.)

Instructions regarding War Diaries and Intelligence Summaries are contained in F. S. Regs., Part II. and the Staff Manual respectively. Title Pages will be prepared in manuscript.

Place	Date	Hour	Summary of Events and Information	Remarks and references to Appendices
In the field	24/1/17		Arranged for Co. Working with 17 M.G. Coy. Men working on usual routine of fatigue work. Weather fine & frosty.	
		9.0 pm to 1.0 am (25.1.17)	Indirect fire on German ration dumps, new area, & roads	
In the field	25/1/17		Weather fine & frosty.	
		10.30	Met O/C 64 M.G. Coy. Inspected emplacements with him & made arrangements for handing over. O/C 73 M.G. Coy paid to report at Commandant's office.	
			Indirect fire on German truck area, ration dumps & roads.	
In the field	26/1/17	10.0 pm 6.45 am	Indirect fire in connection with 17 M.G. Coy during night. Fine frosty. Visit from C.O. Inspected guns. Visited O/C 64 M.G. Coy re handing over. Company on usual routine work.	
		6.0 pm to 7.0 am (27/1/17)	Indirect fire on German new area, ration dumps & roads.	

2449 Wt. W14957/M90 750,000 1/16 J.B.C. & A. Forms/C.2118/12.

Army Form C. 2118.

WAR DIARY
or
INTELLIGENCE SUMMARY

(Erase heading not required.)

191 M.G. Coy

Place	Date	Hour	Summary of Events and Information	Remarks and references to Appendices
In the field	27/1/17	10·0pm	Fine. Frosty. Men on repairing emplacements, cleaning trenches. Indirect fire on German new area, ration dumps.	
In the field	28/1/17	10·0pm to 12 MID night	Fine frosty. Men on repairing emplacements & dug outs, cleaning trenches. Indirect fire on German rear area ration dumps roads.	
In the field	29/1/17		Fine frosty. Men repairing dug outs & emplacements, cleaning trenches & general routine work.	
In the field	30/1/17	10·0pm to 2·0am (31/1/17)	Cold & a little snow. Men on usual fatigues & routine work. Indirect fire on German rear area, ration dumps & roads. Enemy limbers heard galloping down road.	

Army Form C. 2118.

191: M.G. Coy

WAR DIARY
or
INTELLIGENCE SUMMARY

(Erase heading not required.)

Place	Date	Hour	Summary of Events and Information	Remarks and references to Appendices
In the Field	31/1/17		Visit Maisnigarde. Interview at Brigade Headqrs. Rapid transport men on Routine work, repairing emplacements, trenches &c.	

C.J.Cross Capt
O/c 191 M.G. Coy

Army Form C. 2118.

191. Machine Gun Coy.
Vol 3

WAR DIARY or INTELLIGENCE SUMMARY
(Erase heading not required.)

Place	Date	Hour	Summary of Events and Information	Remarks and references to Appendices
In the Field	1/2/17		Frosty. Trench repairing Hatchetts Corner. Repairing indirect firing position English Alley.	
		9pm	Indirect fire on enemy rear area.	
In the Field	2/2/17		Frosty. Building Headquarters accommodation for clerks & Lewisville. Repairing trench at A5 & Tram dugout C2.	
In the Field	3/2/17		Frosty. B7 emplacement damaged by enemy shell fire. Making new dug outs B5, & B7. Building new emplacements in Gloucester Lane. Repairing trench near A5. H.Q. accommodation.	
In the Field	4/2/17		Frosty. Church Parade Mazingarbe. Salvage. H.Q. accommodation. Building new dug out B5. Repairing B7 emplacement.	Trench repairs A5.
In the Field	5/2/17	9.0 pm to 12.0 midnight	Frosty. Salvage work. H.Q. accommodation. Repairing B7 emplacement. Indirect fire on enemy rear area.	
In the Field	6/2/17		Frosty. Salvage work. H.Q. accommodation. Repairing B7 emplacement.	

Army Form C. 2118.

WAR DIARY
or
INTELLIGENCE SUMMARY
(Erase heading not required.)

191- Machine Gun Coy

Place	Date	Hour	Summary of Events and Information	Remarks and references to Appendices
In the Field	7/2/17		Frosty. Visited Maysingarde. Inspected Transport. Visited Noeux les mines. Inspected detachment. Company on Salvage work. H.Q. accommodation.	
		10.0 pm 2.0 am 8/2/17	Enemy trench A5. New dug out B5. Enemy fire on enemy rear areas & ration dumps	
In the Field	8/2/17		Frosty. Repairing roof of us Hd Qrs. Repairing loop hold A3. Salvage work. H.Q accommodation.	
In the Field	9/2/17	8pm 12 midn?	Frosty. Building A7 emplacement. repairing trenches. Enemy fire on enemy rear areas & ration dumps.	
In the Field	10/2/17.		Frosty. Visited Maysingarde. Interviewed Brigade. Inspected transport & Q.M. stores. Visited Noeux les mines & inspected detachment. Company on Salvage work. repairing trenches & emplacements.	
In the Field	11/2/17	12 midn? 4 am 11/2/17.	Frosty. Repairing Trenches. clearing A5 trench. Building new dug out for Head Quarters. Enemy fire on enemy rear areas & ration dumps.	

Army Form C. 2118.

191. M.G. Coy

WAR DIARY
or
INTELLIGENCE SUMMARY

(Erase heading not required.)

Instructions regarding War Diaries and Intelligence Summaries are contained in F.S. Regs., Part II. and the Staff Manual respectively. Title Pages will be prepared in manuscript.

Place	Date	Hour	Summary of Events and Information	Remarks and references to Appendices
In the Field	12/4/17		Thaw. Repairing trenches, emplacements & dugouts. New dugout for HQrs.	
In the Field	13/4/17	9.0pm 2.0pm (14/4/17)	Thaw. Repairing trenches, emplacements, dugouts. Indirect fire on enemy near pasture station dumps.	
In the Field	14/4/17		Thaw. Repairing trenches, emplacements & dugouts.	
In the Field	15/4/17		Thaw. Repairing emplacements, trenches & dugouts.	
In the Field	16/4/17		Thaw. Cleaning up all emplacements & preparing to move.	
In the Field	17/4/17		Thaw. Relieved by 112 M.G. Coy. Relief complete 8 p.m. Company arrived at Behin 11.0pm.	
In the Field	18/4/17	7.0 p.m.	Fine. Company moved to ALLOUAGNE. Train by 79 CMF 10861. Pte Adams J. at MAZINGARBE. Coy arrived ALLOUAGNE.	

Army Form C. 2118.

WAR DIARY
or
INTELLIGENCE SUMMARY

(Erase heading not required.)

191 M. G. Coy

Instructions regarding War Diaries and Intelligence Summaries are contained in F. S. Regs., Part II. and the Staff Manual respectively. Title Pages will be prepared in manuscript.

Place	Date	Hour	Summary of Events and Information	Remarks and references to Appendices
In the Field	19/2/17		Fine. Company Resting. Machine Gun Training.	
In the Field	20/2/17		Well. Company Resting. Machine Gun Training	
In the Field	21/2/17		Fine. Company Resting. Machine Gun Training	
In the Field	22/2/17		Wet. Company Resting. Machine Gun Training. 15 men reported from Base.	
In the Field	23/2/17		Fine. Company Resting. Machine Gun Training. 2nd Lt. H.Q. Inkerman reported for duty from Base. Promulgation of sentence of F.G.C.M. case of 1086 Pte Adams J.	
In the Field	24/2/17		Fine. Company Resting. Machine Gun Training	
In the Field	25/2/17		Fine. Company Resting. Machine Gun Training.	
In the Field	26/2/17		Fine. Company Resting. Machine Gun Training.	
In the Field	27/2/17		Fine. Company Resting. Machine gun Training. 1 man reported from base.	

Army Form C. 2118.

WAR DIARY
or
INTELLIGENCE SUMMARY

(Erase heading not required.)

191 M.G. Coy

Instructions regarding War Diaries and Intelligence Summaries are contained in F.S. Regs., Part II. and the Staff Manual respectively. Title Pages will be prepared in manuscript.

Place	Date	Hour	Summary of Events and Information	Remarks and references to Appendices
In the Field	28/2/17		Company resting. Machine Gun training.	

C. J. Cross Capt.
Commanding 191 M.G. Coy

Army Form C. 2118.

WAR DIARY
or
INTELLIGENCE SUMMARY

(Erase heading not required.)

191. M. G. Coy.   Vol "4"

Place	Date	Hour	Summary of Events and Information	Remarks and references to Appendices
In the Field	1/3/17	Fine.	Company resting. Musketry.	
In the Field	2/3/17	Fine	Company resting. Musketry.	
In the Field	3/3/17	Fine	Company resting. Musketry.	
In the Field	4/3/17	Snow.	Company resting. Musketry.	
In the Field	5/3/17	Fine	Company resting. Musketry.	
In the Field	6/3/17	Fine	Company resting. Musketry.	
In the Field	7/3/17	Fine	Company resting. Musketry.	
In the Field	8/3/17	Fine	Company resting. Musketry.	
In the Field	9/3/17	Fine	Company resting. Musketry.	
In the Field	10/3/17	Fine	Company resting. Musketry.	
In the Field	11/3/17	Fine	Company resting. Preparing to return to the line.	
In the Field	12/3/17	Unsettled	40 men of Company in Musketry. Irregret Parade line with G.S.O.III sitting M.G. Positions. Company moves to Margueffles Farm. 40 men left behind under Lieut J.H. Hansen to continue musketry	

Army Form C. 2118.

WAR DIARY
or
INTELLIGENCE SUMMARY

(Erase heading not required.)

191. M.G. Coy.

Place	Date	Hour	Summary of Events and Information	Remarks and references to Appendices
In the Field	13/3/17		Fine. Siting M.G. positions with G.S.O. III. Company cleaning guns limbers &c. Detached party Musketry.	
In the Field	14/3/17		Fine. Siting M.G. positions with G.S.O. III. Company carrying on with M.G. drill & gas helmet drill. Detached party of Musketry.	
In the Field	15/3/17		Unsettled. Move tour of MAESTRE LINE. with Section Officers, explained defence. Company. M.G. drill & gas helmet drill. Detached party Musketry.	
In the Field	16/3/17		Fair. Siting M.G. positions with G.S.O. III. Company building Emplacements 100 & 104. Detached party Musketry.	
In the Field	17/3/17		Fair. Siting M.G. positions with G.S.O. III. Men working on Emplacements 100 & 104 & dug out. Detached party Musketry.	
In the Field	18/3/17		Interview O/C Sherwood Forests re supplying Pioneers. Coy working on Emplacements & dug out 100 & 101. Detached party rejoin Company.	

Army Form C. 2118.

WAR DIARY
or
INTELLIGENCE SUMMARY

(Erase heading not required.)

191. M.G. Coy.

Place	Date	Hour	Summary of Events and Information	Remarks and references to Appendices
In the Field	19/3/17		Unsettled. Visit line, & Company to work on various emplacements. Interview C.R.E.	
In the Field	20/3/17		Unsettled. Company working on M.G. emplacements.	
In the Field	21/3/17		Fine. Inspect line with Major Smith (R.E. 104 Coy).	
In the Field	22/3/17		Fine. Tour of line with section officers. Defence scheme.	
In the Field	23/3/17		Unsettled. Company working on M.G. emplacements.	
In the Field	24/3/17		Unsettled. Company working on M.G. emplacements & shelters	
In the Field	25/3/17		Fair. Company working on M.G. Emplacements & shelters	
In the Field	26/3/17		Fair. Artillery/Infantry & Inf. Addresses at H.Q. of 157 & 158 Bde. Company working on M.G. Emplacements & shelters	
In the Field	27/3/17		Fair. Selecting further M.G positions with G.S.O.III. Company working on M.G Emplacements & shelters	
In the Field	28/3/17		Fine. Visit Headqrs. 97 Inf Bde. to meet Major Morgan R.E. Inspect various positions & siting reports. Company working on M.G. Emplacements & shelters	

Army Form C. 2118.

WAR DIARY
or
INTELLIGENCE SUMMARY

191 M.G. Coy

IV

(Erase heading not required.)

Instructions regarding War Diaries and Intelligence Summaries are contained in F. S. Regs., Part II. and the Staff Manual respectively. Title Pages will be prepared in manuscript.

Place	Date	Hour	Summary of Events and Information	Remarks and references to Appendices
In the Field	29/3/17		Sect. Tour of MAISTRE LINE with guides & inspected position of each emplacement. Company working on M.G. emplacements & shelters.	
In the Field	30/3/17		Interview between CRE & G.S.O.III. Company working on emplacements & shelters.	
In the Field	31/3/17		Interview. Company working on emplacements & shelters.	

C.J. Ards Capt.
Commanding 191 M.G. Coy

191st MACHINE GUN COMPANY

24th DIVISION

APRIL 1917

Army Form C. 2118.

190 Machine Gun Coy

Vol 3

WAR DIARY
or
INTELLIGENCE SUMMARY

(Erase heading not required.)

Place	Date	Hour	Summary of Events and Information	Remarks and references to Appendices
In the Field	1/4/17		Unsettled. Met Major Trojan R.E. & 17. Inf. Bgde Hqrs. Visit MAISTRE LINE with him selecting positions for emg. outs. Attend Divisional Headquarters. met G.S.O.III & 1st Corps M.G. Officer & Canadian Corps M.G. Officer. Company working in MAISTRE LINE on emplacements & shelters.	
In the Field	2/4/17		Snow. Company working on emplacements & shelters in the MAISTRE LINE	
In the Field	3/4/17		Thaw. Visit LORETTE SPUR with C/Sergt Major & a Corporal in charge of guides for MAISTRE LINE positions. Company working on MAISTRE LINE. on emplacements & shelters.	
In the Field	4/4/17		Fine Dull. Company working on emplacement & shelters in MAISTRE LINE	

Army Form C. 2118.

WAR DIARY
or
INTELLIGENCE SUMMARY

191st Machine Gun Coy

(Erase heading not required.)

Instructions regarding War Diaries and Intelligence Summaries are contained in F. S. Regs., Part II. and the Staff Manual respectively. Title Pages will be prepared in manuscript.

Place	Date	Hour	Summary of Events and Information	Remarks and references to Appendices
In the Field	5/4/17		Fine. Visit O/c 73 M.G. Coy with reference to handing operations. Company working on Emplacements & shelters in MAISTRE LINE	
In the Field	6/4/17		Fine. Two teams relieve 2 teams of 73rd M.G. Coy. attached to 73rd M.G. Coy. Remainder of Company working on emplacements & shelters in MAISTRE line	
In the Field	7/4/17		Fine. Visit 73rd Inf Bgde Headqrs. re my attachments during operations. 2 teams report over to 73rd M.G. Coy & became attached that Company for operations. Remainder of Company working on emplacements & shelters in MAISTRE line.	
In the Field	8/4/17		Fine. Four teams sent to 73rd M.G. Coy & became attached to them for operations. Remainder of Company working at emplacements & shelters in MAISTRE line	

2449 Wt. W14957/M90 750,000 1/16 J.B.C. & A.   Forms/C.2118/12.

Army Form C. 2118.

WAR DIARY
or
INTELLIGENCE SUMMARY
(Erase heading not required.)

191st Machine Gun Coy

Instructions regarding War Diaries and Intelligence Summaries are contained in F. S. Regs., Part II. and the Staff Manual respectively. Title Pages will be prepared in manuscript.

Place	Date	Hour	Summary of Events and Information	Remarks and references to Appendices
In the Field	9/4/17		Unsettled. 6 guns & teams in reserve at MARQUEFFLES farm.	
In the Field	10/4/17		Unsettled. Some Snow. 6 guns & teams in reserve at MARQUEFFLES farm. 36265 Sgt PLACE J. killed near AIX NOULETTE Church by hostile shell.	
In the Field	11/4/17		Snow. 6 guns in reserve at MARQUEFFLES farm. 17 Other ranks report for duty. I report to 73 Inf Bgde H.Qrs. & remain during operations.	
In the Field	12/4/17		Snow. 6 guns in reserve at MARQUEFFLES farm. 2nd Lt. Hoffman reports from Divisional School	
In the Field	13/4/17	12·noon	Return from 73 Inf Bgde Headquarters to Coy. 2nd Lt. James returns from 24th Divisional School	

Army Form C. 2118.

WAR DIARY
or
INTELLIGENCE SUMMARY

191st Machine Gun Coy

(Erase heading not required.)

Place	Date	Hour	Summary of Events and Information	Remarks and references to Appendices
In the Field	14/4/17		Unsettled. 8 guns & teams return from 73rd M.G. Coy. Company concentrates at MARQUEFFLES FARM	
In the Field	15/4/17		Rain. Company road making in ANGRES.	
In the Field	16/4/17		Rain. Company road making in ANGRES.	
In the Field	17/4/17		Rain Storms. Company on M.G. work at MARQUEFFLES Farm. 2nd Lt A. Howie & 2 gun teams return from 72nd M.G. Coy.	
In the Field	18/4/17		Rain. Company road making near ANGRES	
In the Field	19/4/17		Unsettled. Company preparing to move into rest.	
In the Field	20/4/17	9.00 am	Fine. Leave MARQUEFFLES FARM for ALLOUAGNE. Men in billets at 3.10 pm.	

Army Form C. 2118.

WAR DIARY
or
INTELLIGENCE SUMMARY

191st Machine Gun Coy

(Erase heading not required.)

Place	Date	Hour	Summary of Events and Information	Remarks and references to Appendices
In the Field	21/4/17	9.0 am	Fine. Company proceed to NORRENTTE FONTES. Billeted at 1.45. pm	
In the Field	22/4/17	9.30.	Fine. Church Parade.	
In the Field	23/4/17		Fine. Company washing limbers & preparing to move.	
In the Field	24/4/17	10.0 4.0 4.15	Fine. Leave NORRENTTE FONTES. Arrive RUPIGNY. Company in Billets.	
In the Field	25/4/17		Fine. Company perform 1 hrs drill. Resting.	
In the Field	26/4/17	9.0 1.30	Fine. I report to Divisional Headquarters. Receive orders to move. Motor to LILLERS & arrange relief with O.C. 54. M.G. Coy. Company leave RUPIGNY for the following Anti aircraft Dix work. LAPUGNOY (3 guns) TREZIENNES (2 guns). ST VENANT (2 guns) ROBECQ (2 guns). Company Headqrs Tommerry of Coy at LE PINE. near LILLERS. all reliefs complete at 9.30 pm	

2449 Wt. W14957/Mg0 750,000 1/16 J.B.C. & A. Forms/C.2118/12.

Army Form C. 2118.

WAR DIARY
or
INTELLIGENCE SUMMARY

(Erase heading not required.)

Instructions regarding War Diaries and Intelligence Summaries are contained in F. S. Regs., Part II. and the Staff Manual respectively. Title Pages will be prepared in manuscript.

Place	Date	Hour	Summary of Events and Information	Remarks and references to Appendices
In the Field	27/4/17	Fine.	Parr Company resting. Remainder on Anti Aircraft work.	
In the Field	28/4/17	Fine.	Visit St VENANT & ROBECQ. inspecting guns & transport. Parr Company on Anti Aircraft work. Remainder on Machine Gun drill & training.	
In the Field	29/4/17	Fine.	Visit LAPUGNOY. inspecting guns & transport. Parr Company on Anti Aircraft work. Remainder on Machine Gun training.	
In the Field	30/4/17	Fine	Parr Company on Anti Aircraft work. Remainder on Machine Gun training.	

C. S. Cross Capt.
Commanding 191st M.G. Co.

191st Machine Gun Coy.

Army Form C. 2118.

WAR DIARY
or
INTELLIGENCE SUMMARY.
(Erase heading not required.)

Vol 6

Instructions regarding War Diaries and Intelligence Summaries are contained in F. S. Regs., Part II. and the Staff Manual respectively. Title pages will be prepared in manuscript.

Place	Date	Hour	Summary of Events and Information	Remarks and references to Appendices
In the Field	1/5/17		Fine. Visit Anti aircraft positions with Corpo M.G.O. Company on anti aircraft duty.	
In the Field	2/5/17		Fine. Company on anti aircraft duty.	
In the Field	3/5/17		Fine. Company on anti aircraft duty.	
In the Field	4/5/17		Fine. Company on anti aircraft duty.	
In the Field	5/5/17		Fine. Company on anti aircraft duty.	
In the Field	6/5/17		Fine. Company on anti aircraft duty.	
In the Field	7/5/17		Fine. Company on anti aircraft duty.	
In the Field	8/5/17		Fine. Company on anti aircraft duty.	

Army Form C. 2118.

191st Machine Gun Coy.

WAR DIARY
or
INTELLIGENCE SUMMARY.
(Erase heading not required.)

Instructions regarding War Diaries and Intelligence Summaries are contained in F.S. Regs., Part II. and the Staff Manual respectively. Title pages will be prepared in manuscript.

Place	Date	Hour	Summary of Events and Information	Remarks and references to Appendices
In the Field	9/5/17		Fine. Company moves to THIENNES	
In the Field	10/5/17		Fine. Routine work. Preparing for Inspection.	
In the Field	11/5/17		Fine. Inspection by G.O.C. 24th Div.	
In the Field	12/5/17		Fine. Moves from THIENNES to STEENVORDE.	
In the Field	13/5/17		Fine. Routine work	
In the Field	14/5/17		Fine. Preparing to move. Machine limbers &c.	
In the Field	15/5/17		Fine. Moves from STEENVORDE to LES CISEAUX.	
In the Field	16/5/17		Fine. Moves from LES CISEAUX to ZEVECOTEN.	
In the Field	17/5/17		Fine. Coy building emplacements in the line	
In the Field	18/5/17		Fine. Coy building emplacements in the line	
In the Field	19/5/17		Fine. Coy building emplacements in the line	
In the Field	20/5/17		Fine. Visit Corps M.G.O. with M.G.O. 41st Div. Coy building emplacements in line	
In the Field	21/5/17		Fine. Coy building emplacements in line. 7037/536 Pte LEWIS wounded	
In the Field	22/5/17		Wet. Coy building emplacements in the line, & carrying up ammunition	
In the Field	23/5/17		Fine. Coy building emplacement in the line. 7037/402 Cpl WILLIAMS wounded.	
In the Field	24/5/17		Fine. Visit Corps M.G.O. with M.G.O 41st Div. Coy building emplacement & carrying ammunition to the line	

191st Machine Gun Coy. Army Form C. 2118.

WAR DIARY
or
INTELLIGENCE SUMMARY.
(Erase heading not required.)

Place	Date	Hour	Summary of Events and Information	Remarks and references to Appendices
In the Field	25/5/17		Fine. Coy building emplacements & carrying ammunition up the line.	
In the Field	26/5/17		Fine. Coy building emplacement & carrying ammunition up the line.	
In the Field	27/5/17		Fine. Coy carrying ammunition up the line	
In the Field	28/5/17		Fine. Coy carrying ammunition up the line	
In the Field	29/5/17		Fine. Coy carrying ammunition up the line. 103978, Pte Shevers F. wounded.	
In the Field	30/5/17		Fine. Coy carrying ammunition up the line	
In the Field	31/5/17		Fine. Coy carrying ammunition up the line	

C. J. Cross Capt.
O/c 191st M.G. Coy.

CONFIDENTIAL.

24th Division No. M.132.

D. A. G.,
   3rd Echelon,
     Base.

      Herewith please find War Diary for the month of JUNE for the 191st Machine Gun Company.

July 17th 1917.

                 Major General,
       Commanding 24th Division.

Army Form C. 2118.

191st Machine Gun Company

WAR DIARY
or
INTELLIGENCE SUMMARY.
(Erase heading not required.)

Instructions regarding War Diaries and Intelligence Summaries are contained in F. S. Regs., Part II. and the Staff Manual respectively. Title pages will be prepared in manuscript.

Place	Date	Hour	Summary of Events and Information	Remarks and references to Appendices
In the Field	1/6/17		Line. Company working on Machine Gun emplacements etc. near Ypres canal.	
"	2/6/17		Line. Company working on Machine Gun emplacements and carrying ammunition to dump near Shelley Farm.	
"	3/6/17		Line. Company carrying ammunition to dump near Shelley Farm.	
"	4/6/17		Line. Company carrying ammunition to dump near Shelley Farm.	
"	5/6/17		Line. Company carrying ammunition to dump near Shelley Farm.	
"	6/6/17		Line. Company overhauling machine guns, equipment, belts, ammunition etc. Thoroughly cleaning and testing guns.	
"	7/6/17		Line. Company resting until 7.0 p.m. 7.0 p.m. Company leave Reninghelst for Woesten. Arrive at 10.0 p.m. Company proceed to Assembly positions near Shelley Farm.	
"	8/6/17	3.10 a.m.	Line. Action commences. Company divided into two batteries viz: "Y" and "Z". Each battery consisting of 8 guns.	
"		3.30 a.m.	"Y" and "Z" Batteries move forward to positions "Y" and "Z" for barrage to cover advance against Black line and escort in defence of Blue line. Movement completed by 4.30 a.m.	

2353 Wt. W2544/1454 700,000 5/15 D. D. & L. A.D.S.S./Forms/C. 2118.

Army Form C. 2118.

WAR DIARY
or
INTELLIGENCE SUMMARY.

(Erase heading not required.)

191st Machine Gun Company

Place	Date	Hour	Summary of Events and Information	Remarks and references to Appendices
In the Field	8/6/17		Each gun had its Zero line worked out beforehand for each position. On arriving at a new position, the Officer Commanding the battery went forward and took a back bearing on the gun, which at the same time laid on him. He then ordered it to be tapped so many degrees to the right or left in order to get its Zero direction. Holes were filled in, sheet holes behind the batteries.	
		8.50 a.m.	"Y" and "Z" Batteries move to "Y3" and "Z3" positions covering barrage to gun line and its subsequent protection. No difficulty was experienced in finding these positions. On these positions the batteries were heavily shelled. 2nd Lieut. D. Jenkins who was Commanding "Z" Battery, was on two occasions blown up with his guns by heavy shells, but he dug them out and got them into action on each occasion. He showed a splendid example to his men. Casualties 13 men wounded.	
	9/6/17		Fine. Company consolidating positions. Subjected to irregular shell fire. Casualties 1 man wounded.	

Army Form C. 2118.

WAR DIARY
or
INTELLIGENCE SUMMARY.

(Erase heading not required.)

191st Machine Gun Company

Instructions regarding War Diaries and Intelligence Summaries are contained in F.S. Regs., Part II. and the Staff Manual respectively. Title pages will be prepared in manuscript.

Place	Date	Hour	Summary of Events and Information	Remarks and references to Appendices
In the Field	10/6/17		Company holding positions gained. Shelling very little.	
"	11/6/17		Company relieved. Assembled at Vootsuyzeele. Returned to Reninghelst.	
	12/6/17		Company inspected by G.O.C. 34th Division. Company cleaning stores, guns and material. Preparing for move to camp near Dickebusch.	
	13/6/17		Company moved camp from Reninghelst to near Dickebusch. Camp erected near Windmill. Company resting.	
	14/6/17		Company training. Physical training. Elementary Machine Gun drill. Immediate action etc. Packing and washing limbers etc.	
	15/6/17		Training continued. Physical training. Advanced Machine Gun drill, immediate action etc.	
	16/6/17		Training continued. Physical training. Advanced Machine Gun drill. Cleaning ammunition. Sections preparing to go into line at Hill 60 and near Larchwood.	
	17/6/17		2 sections in line. Remainder Company Church Parade.	

Army Form C. 2118.

WAR DIARY
or
INTELLIGENCE SUMMARY.

(Erase heading not required.)

191st Machine Gun Company

Place	Date	Hour	Summary of Events and Information	Remarks and references to Appendices
In the Field	18/6/17	Fine.	2 Sections in line. Heavily shelled.	
"	19/6/17	Showery	2 Sections Training. Physical drill, Arms drill, Gun cleaning etc. 2 Sections in line. Fairly heavy shelling by enemy.	
"	20/6/17	Fine.	2 Sections training.	
"	21/6/17	Fine.	2 Sections in line relieved and return to Company Headquarters near Dickebusch. 2 Sections in line. Physical training.	
"	22/6/17	Fine.	Machine Gun Drill, cleaning Gun parts etc.	
"	23/6/17	Wet.	2 Sections in line. Intermittent shelling.	
"	23/6/17	Fine.	2 Sections continue training in camp.	
"	24/6/17	Fine.	2 Sections in line. 2 Sections continue training in camp.	
"	25/6/17	Fine.	2 Sections in line. 2 Sections rest in camp.	
"	26/6/17	Fine.	2 Sections in line relieved and return to Company Headquarters near Dickebusch. 2 Sections training. Physical training, Machine Gun Drill, cleaning Gun parts. O.C. visits Cassel to see Camp Commandant	

Army Form C. 2118.

WAR DIARY
or
INTELLIGENCE SUMMARY.

(Erase heading not required.)

191st Machine Gun Company

Instructions regarding War Diaries and Intelligence Summaries are contained in F. S. Regs., Part II. and the Staff Manual respectively. Title pages will be prepared in manuscript.

Place	Date	Hour	Summary of Events and Information	Remarks and references to Appendices
In the Field	26/6/17	Fine	3 Sections in line. 2 Sections continue training in Camp.	
"	27/6/17	Fine	2 Sections in line. Heavily shelled. 3 Sections continue training.	
"	28/6/17	Fine	3 Sections in line. 2 Sections continue training in Camp.	
"	29/6/17	Fine	2 Sections relieved and return to Company Headquarters near Wiskebrook. Preparations for Camp moving.	
"	30/6/17	Wet	Company proceeds to Cassel to take up Anti-aircraft duties for the protection of H.M. The King.	

C. J. Croll. Capt.
O.C. 191st Machine Gun Company.

Army Form C. 2118.

WAR DIARY
or
INTELLIGENCE SUMMARY.
(Erase heading not required.)

191st Machine Gun Company

Vol 8

Place	Date	Hour	Summary of Events and Information	Remarks and references to Appendices
In the Field	1/7/17	Fine	Company at Carel on Anti-Aircraft duty. Established as follows:- 4 Guns in reserve. (O.6.C.3.3.) 8 Guns at P.1.d.9.3. 4 Guns at O.5.d.3.3. (Sheet 27)	
"	2/7/17	Fine	Company at Carel on Anti-Aircraft defences. 2/Lt. Wilmot being evacuated to base is struck off strength. No. 37944 L/Cpl. Sweeton R. returned to duty from hospital. G.R.O. No. 295. Firearm certificates published a arms.	
"	3/7/17	Fine	Company at Carel on Anti-Aircraft defences. H.M. Stirling arrives.	
"	4/7/17	Fine	Company at Carel on Anti-Aircraft defences. The following N.C.O's and men struck off strength owing to them having been evacuated to U.K. No. 42064 L/Sgt. Chapman T. 36777 L/Sgt. Ellis R. 58763 Pte. Fenton W. 27956 Pte. Andrews H. 42039. Sgt. Woodall A. reported from base depot.	
"	5/7/17	Fine	Company at Carel on Anti-Aircraft defences. No. W.H. Blyth attached to the unit.	
"	6/7/17	Showery	Company at Carel on Anti-Aircraft defences.	
"	7/7/17	Fine	Company at Carel on Anti-Aircraft defences. H.M. Stirling leaves Carel. No.58380 Cpl. Freeman J.A. 71903 Pte. Martin J. were discharged from hospital. Lieut. J.N. Hanson proceeded on leave to U.K.	

WAR DIARY
or
INTELLIGENCE SUMMARY.
(Erase heading not required.)

Army Form C. 2118.

191st Machine Gun Coy BEF

Place	Date	Hour	Summary of Events and Information	Remarks and references to Appendices
In the Field	8/7/17	9.20 AM	Showery. Company moved from Casel to Lumbres by motor lorries. Arriving at Lumbres 10-30 am	
"	9/7/17		Fine. Company in training. Physical training, Elementary Machine Gun drill Mechanism, Immediate action	
"	10/7/17		Fine. Company in training. Physical training, Elementary Machine Gun drill Mechanism, Immediate action. No 58391 Pte Blackburn C. admitted to hospital. No 42009 L/Cpl Hirst J. becomes attached to 234th Employment Coy. and is struck of the strength of the unit.	
"	11/7/17		Fine. Company in training. Physical training, Elementary Machine Gun drill Mechanism, Immediate action etc. 2/Lieut SPV Noble admitted to hospital. G.R.O. 2424 7/7/17. "Censorship" published in orders. 89684 Pte Brown M. admitted hospital	
"	12/7/17		Fine. Company in training. Practising advancing over open country establishing batteries. Lying out lines of fire. 58862 Pte Grundy J. 82035 Pte MacCarral R. admitted hospital.	

Army Form C. 2118.

WAR DIARY
or
INTELLIGENCE SUMMARY.
(Erase heading not required.)

191st Machine Gun Company

Place	Date	Hour	Summary of Events and Information	Remarks and references to Appendices
In the Field	13/7/17	Fine	Company training continued. 58578 Pte Ramage C. 84186 McClean W. 81571 Pte Patmore E. Admitted Hospital. 25987 Pte Kelly J. remanded for Field General Court Martial.	
"	14/7/17	Showery Thunder	Company training continued. 58601 Pte Bowen. 55195 Pte Hutton T. Admitted Hospital.	
"	15/7/17	Fine	Church parade 9.30 a.m. 53597 Pte Rae J. 53075 Pte Ewentree C. to Hospital.	
"	16/7/17	Fine	Company training continued. 25987 Pte Kelly J. tried by F.G.C.M. 59410 Pte Whitehead W. to the Base Corps (umpire). 58760 L/Cpl Willey P. 44057 Pte Lamphere B. 84059 Pte Lender G. Admitted Hospital. 55195 Pte Hutton T. struck off strength.	
"	17/7/17	Fine	Preparing to move. Packing and washing limbers. Cleaning up Sidcot, transport lines etc.	
"	18/7/17	Wet	Company moved to Le Nippe (Sheet 27) U.6.C.4.2. Commenced from Limbres 4.15 a.m. arrived at billets at 11 a.m. 2/Lt H.H. Robinson, 2/Lt H.E. Webb report for duty. 64821 Pte Dixon H. admitted to Hospital.	

2353 Wt W2314/1454 700,000 5/15 L.D. & L.   A.D.S.S./Forms/C. 2118.

Army Form C. 2118.

WAR DIARY
or
INTELLIGENCE SUMMARY.
(Erase heading not required.)

191st Machine Gun Company

Place	Date	Hour	Summary of Events and Information	Remarks and references to Appendices
In the Field	19/7/17		Line Company moved to Cache Area. (Sheet 27) V.H.C.3.5. Commenced from Le Nippe at 5.15 a.m. Arrived in billets at 8.0 p.m. Lieut. Anderson M.C. proceeds on leave. Lieut. J.H. Hansen returns from leave. C.Q.M.S. Thompson returns from leave. 10314 Pte Bostock is admitted to hospital. 36803 Sgt Macey J. appointed C.Q.M.S. of No. 7. M.G. Coy and is struck off strength of the unit. Proceedings of F.G.C.M. on 25787 Pte Kelly J promulgated. Imprisonment awarded 90 days F.P. No1.	
"	23/7/17		Line Company moved to Eeke Area (Sheet 27) Q.27.8.1.8 No. 36804 A/Sgt Smith A.H. promoted Sergeant from 14/6/17. No. 58380 A/Cpl Freeman J.W. promoted Corporal from 4/6/17.	
"	27/7/17		Line Company moved to Runningelst Area (Sheet 28) G.22.C.8.7. 5735.97 Pte Rae J. 16977. Pte Grundy J struck off strength 10 Guns taken over in line from 69th & 70th M.G.Coys "B" & "C" Batteries. 2 Sergeants 2 Corporals report from Base Depot.	

Army Form C. 2118.

WAR DIARY
or
INTELLIGENCE SUMMARY.
(Erase heading not required.)

191st Machine Gun Coy.

Place	Date	Hour	Summary of Events and Information	Remarks and references to Appendices
Lille Field	23/9/17		Fine. 10 Guns in line. Company moved from H.32.c.5.5. Lieut C.H. Brook struck off strength unfit to return. Awaiting M.B. Gun Positions at :- 2 Guns at I.29.d.80.50. 4 Guns at I.28.d.35.80. 4 Guns at I.28.d.65.95. "B" Battery. Casualties Nil S.A.A. Expenditure 60,000 Rds. Situation Normal. "C" Battery. Casualties Nil. S.A.A. Expenditure 6,000 Rds. Situation Normal. one gun slightly damaged by shell fire.	
"	24/9/17		Fine. "B" Battery. Casualties Nil S.A.A. Expenditure Nil Situation Normal. Harassing fire on account of friendly raid. Positions heavily shelled with new mustard gas. "C" Battery. Casualties Nil S.A.A. Expenditure 3000 Rds. Situation Normal.	
"	25/9/17		Fine. "B" Battery. Casualties Nil S.A.A. Expenditure 6,000 Rds. Situation Normal. "C" Battery. Casualties Nil S.A.A. Expended 10,000 Rds. Situation Normal. Harassing fire from position at J.25.c.7.0. to J.31.a.60.7.0. Covering fire to British raid. From 5. pm to 5.40 pm. Decreased hostile shelling.	

Army Form C. 2118.

WAR DIARY
or
INTELLIGENCE SUMMARY.
(Erase heading not required.)

191st Machine Gun Coy.

Place	Date	Hour	Summary of Events and Information	Remarks and references to Appendices
In the field	26/7/17		"B" Battery. Casualties nil S.A.A. Expenditure 1000 Rds. Situation normal. Firing on enemy lines of communication. "C" Battery. Casualties nil S.A.A. Expenditure 18,000 Rds. Situation normal. Friendly raid at 5 p.m. M.G. Targets = 4 guns location 1.28.d.6.8. on targets at J31.a.8.0. to J31.a.9.5. 2 guns location at 1.29.d.8.5. on targets at J25.d.8.7. to J25.d.8.0. Ammunition dumps completed at "C" position. Trench deepened and gun platforms completed. "B" Battery inapproachable owing to heavy shellfire. 608 H.H. Pte J. Leply W.R. awarded punishment. 21 days F.P. No.1. "When on active service ill-treating a mule."	
	27/7/17		Inter Company relief. "B" Battery. Casualties nil S.A.A. Expended 1000 Rds. Situation normal. Targets from J31.a.8.0. to J31.a.9.5. Gun position 1.28.d.6.8. "C" Battery. Casualties nil S.A.A. Expended nil. Situation normal. 32754 A/Cpl Whaley W. and 15109 A/Cpl Frost N. revert to L/Cpl (unpaid) from 27/7/17 on L/Cpl Smith J. and Cpl Lourmie G.O. joining the company.	

Army Form C. 2118.

19th Machine Gun Corp.

WAR DIARY
or
INTELLIGENCE SUMMARY.
(Erase heading not required.)

Place	Date	Hour	Summary of Events and Information	Remarks and references to Appendices
In the Field	28/7/17	Fine.	"B" Battery Casualties Nil. S.A.A Expenditure Nil. Situation Normal. No harassing fire carried out on night of 27/28 on account of stock on morning of 28th. "C" Battery. Casualties Nil. S.A.A. Expenditure Nil. Situation Normal. The men left the Batteries by gun teams at 11.25 pm at 10 minute intervals for positions for the shoot. All men got cover and the hostile bombardment was very severe until 4 am when it eased slightly. We then mounted and laid all guns returning to No 1 & 2 at the positions. Remaining by guns of the Company form their respective batteries in the line. The move programme of harassing fire was carried out on X/Y night. Roads and lines of communication were heavily shelled by hostile artillery.	
"	29/7/17 "X" DAY	Fine.	All guns and implements taken to positions for operations on "Z" day. "B" Battery at B' position (Sheet 27) I.30.a.05.80. "C" Battery at I.29.D.80.50.	
"	30/7/17 "Y" DAY	Fine.	Advance proceeded to Battery positions during X/Z night. Direction posts laid out. Carrying party remain at previous positions with ammunition to join Batteries at Zero + 2 hrs. 10 minutes.	

Army Form C. 2118

WAR DIARY or INTELLIGENCE SUMMARY

191st Machine Gun Coy.

(Erase heading not required.)

Instructions regarding War Diaries and Intelligence Summaries are contained in F.S. Regs., Part II. and the Staff Manual respectively. Title Pages will be prepared in manuscript.

Place	Date	Hour	Summary of Events and Information	Remarks and references to Appendices
In the field	30/7/17	"Y" Day	Both positions were heavily bombarded during "Y/Z" night.	
	31/7/17	"Z" Day	"Zero" Hour at 3.50 am. Fire opened, and almost immediately was followed by heavy enemy barrage. Enemy machine guns were also very active on "B" position. At 4.10 am left gun "C" Battery knocked out of action by direct hit. Killing Beman and wounding one. Commander "B" Battery is slightly wounded by flying earth but remains at duty. "C" Battery ammunition so set on fire and guns so being buried alternately by hostile artillery fire. These guns, having to be cleaned after each accident leaves it impossible to have more than 4 guns in action simultaneously. Corpl Sutherland ("B" Battery) received bullet wound in afternoon and is sent down to Dressing Station. 5.10 pm All guns cease fire. Battery Commanders and party proceed to reconnoitre second position. ("B" Battery) at J.19.D.35.08. "C" Battery at J.136.B. Central. Lt. James ("B" Battery) with L. Cpl Rice pushed ahead of the remaining personnel who were left in British front line trench under 2/Lt H.E. Webb. At 8.45 a.m. the advance party had not returned, battery therefore went forward and endeavoured to reach B² position but were	

2449 Wt. W14957/Mg0 750,000 1/16 J.B.C. & A. Forms/C.2118/12.

WAR DIARY
or
INTELLIGENCE SUMMARY
(Erase heading not required.)

stopped by very heavy artillery fire. Lieut Herefore came into action at J.19.C.05.05 (Approx) Owing to intensity of shellfire however, firing was impossible and it was decided after conversation between Sub Commander and Battery Sergeant Young (who remained cool and collected throughout this most distressing period) to withdraw guns to 'B' position. It was reported to 2/Lt. Webb that here, Yeoman was wounded, and it was reported to 2/Lt. Webb that R.F. had failed in their first objective. 1 Man of carrying party reported down to atoms. 5 men reported missing and 3 wounded. At 10-15 am. Lieut Jones and 6 O.Ms. Rice returned to 'B' Position having surmised that Battery would have returned there. They reported that in going forward they encountered heavy machine gun fire and were constantly sniped at from various enemy front line which was still occupied by hostile troops. Lieut Jones again assumed command, and acting on instructions received from O.C. prepared to move to second position. Battery (less 2 guns out of action) and with teams considerably weakened, moved forward. The guns and teams lagged in British front line while Battery Commander went E.S.N?

WAR DIARY or INTELLIGENCE SUMMARY

(Erase heading not required.)

Rice went forward to reconnoitre the position. 2.E/M. Rice was here wounded in the face and went down the line. On return of Lieut. James the Battery moved to its second position. Mobile fire had by this time cleared considerably. The ground was in very bad condition and guns were so clogged with mud as to be temporarily useless. Three dug outs were found, two of which were encircle and in good condition. Guns were cleaned and got into action as quickly as possible.

"C" Battery Commander and party proceeded to reconnoitre record position at Zero + 2hrs. 10 minutes. Found dugouts between support and front line. Heavy hostile shelling with large calibre guns proceeding, also M.G. fire and sniping. Men were then sent back for the guns while Commander (Lieut. A. Howie) further reconnoitred. It was found that the position was under direct M.G. and rifle fire from Shrewsbury Forest on left. Mobile fire rendered the manning of guns absolutely impossible and it was decided prudent to withdraw guns and personnel to former position. This was done.

Army Form C. 2

191st Machine Gun Coy.

WAR DIARY
or
INTELLIGENCE SUMMARY
(Erase heading not required.)

Summary of Events and Information

During "Z" day the following twomen did conspicuous service and showed great gallantry in carrying messages several times. Though worn out and under intense fire across the open, all Runners being obliterated, by fire and rain, they succeeded in taking communications between advanced positions, carrying parties, and liason officers. 33929 Pte. Carr. T. 81568 Pte. Pook. C.

C. J. Cross Capt
O.C. 191st M.G. Cn

WAR DIARY
or
INTELLIGENCE SUMMARY

(Erase heading not required.)

Army Form C. 2118.

191st Machine Gun Coy

Vol 9

Place	Date	Hour	Summary of Events and Information	Remarks and references to Appendices
In the Field	1/9/17		Company in line forming two Batteries for Harassing fire on chosen targets and on S.O.S. signal.	
			"B" Battery at I.30.A.05.30. "C" Battery I.29.D.80.50. (Zillebeke map Edition 5A.)	
			"B" Battery :- Apparent hour for S.O.S. fire approximately from 9 a.m. till 12 noon	
			Dusk till midnight and 2 a.m. till Dawn	
			"C" Battery :- Harassing fire carried out on chosen targets. Men are depleted by about 40% by casualties and sickness, consequent on want of sleep and conditions brought about by heavy rains and want of proper shelter.	
	2/8/17		Very Wet. "B" Battery :- Lieut L.D. James sent down the line. (2nd to W.R.) Mobile shellfire particularly heavy. An 18 pdr shell entered the dugout causing 2 casualties.	
			"C" Battery. Owing to expected counter attack imminent warned to be ready to proceed with 2 guns to proximity of I.36.B Central for direct fire if necessary. Intermittent shelling by enemy during the day by light shells and at night by heavy artillery.	
	3/9/17		Showery. "B" Battery. At 7 a.m. 2/Lt H.L.S. Collinson-Jones took command vice	

WAR DIARY
or
INTELLIGENCE SUMMARY

Army Form C. 2118.

191st Machine Gun Coy.

(Erase heading not required.)

Place	Date	Hour	Summary of Events and Information	Remarks and references to Appendices
Battlefield			Lieut. E.D. Davies & 2/Lt. Young with one gun and team sent out to take up wheeled position. Remainder of Battery move to Junction of Jeffrey Avenue and Java Trench. At Jeffrey Avenue remainder of Battery relieved No. 73rd M.G.Coy. At Jeffrey Avenue teams were living in generations in pits of trench with ground waterproof sheets only for covering. There was 2 feet of mud and water in the trench and conditions were very bad indeed. Praise is due to the men for the calm manner in which they accepted these most adverse conditions.	
			"C" Battery :- Hostile Artillery active. Many shells hit trenches and dugouts but no direct hits but remain undamaged. Rumours of counterattack continue but so far none has taken place.	
	4/8/17		Line :- "B" Battery :- 2/Lt. H.G. Williamson relieved 2nd Lt. H.E. Webb to take down the line.	
			"C" Battery :- Relief of Commander and Sub Commander by 2/Lt. L. Anderson, M.C. and 2/Lt. D. Jackson, M.C.	
"	5/8/17		Line :- Casualties Nil. S.A.A. Expended Nil. 100 nors. Situation normal.	

Army Form C. 2118.

WAR DIARY
or
INTELLIGENCE SUMMARY.
(Erase heading not required.)

191st Machine Gun Coy.

Place	Date	Hour	Summary of Events and Information	Remarks and references to Appendices
In the field	5/8/17		Lieut E.D. Jones proceeded to U.K. on leave. 2nd Lt H.N.S. Collinson-Jones to hospital.	
"	6/8/17		Casualties nil. S.A.A. Expended 3,000 rds on targets at J.31.d.2.7 to J.31.b.8.2. Situation normal. Heavy artillery barrage from 9.30 pm to 10.30 pm. Condition of men is becoming very bad. We are suffering from trench feet and exhaustion.	
"	7/8/17		Showery. Casualties nil. S.A.A. Expended 1,000 rds on harassing fire targets J.26.C.0.8 to J.26.C.0.1. Situation normal.	
"	8/8/17		Showery. Casualties nil. S.A.A. Expended 3,000 rds. S.O.S. went up at 9.40 pm. Hostile shelling very heavy from 3.0 am to 6.0 am. At 9.45 pm two green lights were fired in the German line. This was followed by very intense barrage which fell on dug outs and trenches. 11.0 am and 2.0 pm very heavy hostile shelling.	
"	9/8/17		Fine. Casualties nil. S.A.A. Expended 5,000 rds. Situation normal. At 9.45 pm lights were fired from enemy trench followed by heavy barrage fire for 1 hour and 45 minutes.	
"	10/8/17		Fine. Casualties nil. S.A.A. Expended 10,000 rds. from 8.30 pm 9/8/17	

Army Form C. 2118.

WAR DIARY
or
INTELLIGENCE SUMMARY.
(Erase heading not required.)

191st Machine Gun Coy.

Place	Date	Hour	Summary of Events and Information	Remarks and references to Appendices
In the Field	10/8/17		Enemy shelling was incessant, including gas and H.E. shells at 10 p.m. Heavy shelling had ended. At 3.0 p.m. the enemy barrage stopped around the position while we opened our artillery barrage at 4.35 a.m.	
"	11/8/17		Showery. Casualties – S.A.A. Expended 3,000 rds. At 9 p.m. M/g. Heavy shelling was indulged in by enemy including gas shells and 5.9. Desultory shelling continued during the night while H.0.a.m. at flat line. Enemy barrage stopped and continued until 7.0 a.m.	
"	12/8/17		Fire. 2/Lt H.E. Mc. admitted to hospital. 2 Guns mounted on A.A. duties at Divisional H.Q. 1/c 2/Cpl Frost H. 2/Lt. H.H. Robinson relieves 2/Lt. G. Williamson. Lt. A. Howie relieves Lieut D. Anderson M.C. Casualties 293446 Cpl Smith Wounded. S.A.A. Expended 5,500. Heavy Enemy artillery barrage 1-30 a.m. to 3.0 a.m.	
"	13/8/17		Showery. Casualties Nil. Sirs expended. During enemy bombardment a wooden shell attacks to were dugout was destroyed by a direct hit. No men were made, but a quantity of equipment was destroyed.	

Army Form C. 2118.

WAR DIARY
or
INTELLIGENCE SUMMARY.
(Erase heading not required.)

191st Machine Gun Coy.

Instructions regarding War Diaries and Intelligence Summaries are contained in F. S. Regs., Part II. and the Staff Manual respectively. Title pages will be prepared in manuscript.

Place	Date	Hour	Summary of Events and Information	Remarks and references to Appendices
In the Field	13/8/17		Enemy artillery quiet, but aircraft active. Enemy appeared to be bombing the gun pits during the night. Anti-Aircraft report:- Casualties Nil. S.A.A. Expended Nil. No enemy aircraft within range.	
"	14/8/17		Guns Casualties Nil. S.A.A. Expended 8,000 rds. Situation Normal. During day of 13th enemy shelling on our front was very slight. At 9.15 pm enemy put up red, green, and golden flares and opened fire on our line until 9.30 pm. At 4.15 am enemy put down a barrage on our front lasting until 5.15 am and during that period he used a considerable number of mustard gas shells. Large numbers of a.c. were active over our lines the morning. Enemy battery located yesterday on a bearing of 134° mag. from dugout at J.35.B.25.85. Anti-Aircraft report:- Casualties Nil. S.A.A. Expended Nil. No E.A.	
"	15/8/17		Showery. Casualties Nil. S.A.A. Expended 1,750 rds. Situation normal. Heavy enemy shelling between the hours of 10 pm and 11.30 pm on 14th and 12.30 am to 4 am today. Hostile aerial activity during the afternoon.	

Army Form C. 2118.

WAR DIARY
or
INTELLIGENCE SUMMARY. 191st Machine Gun Coy.

(Erase heading not required.)

Instructions regarding War Diaries and Intelligence Summaries are contained in F. S. Regs., Part II. and the Staff Manual respectively. Title pages will be prepared in manuscript.

Place	Date	Hour	Summary of Events and Information	Remarks and references to Appendices
In the Field	15/8/17		Trenches at Shrewsbury Forest were much damaged by enemy artillery.	
"	16/8/17		Fire. 2/Lt. R. Williamson, 2/Lt. O. Jenkins M.C. relieve Lieut. R. Howe and 2/Lt. H.H. Robinson. Casualties 5 wounded. S.A.A. Expended Nil. Situation normal. Enemy artillery quiet during the day. Heavy M.G. and Gas shelling from 1 a.m. to 4.15 a.m. Anti Aircraft report :- Casualties Nil. S.A.A. Expended Nil. No E.A.	
"	17/8/17		Fire. Casualties Nil. S.A.A. Expended Nil. Situation normal. Throughout the day enemy shelling was less active but opened out towards night. Heavy shelling from 1 a.m. to 4.15 a.m. Gas shells were used frequently. Anti Aircraft report :- Casualties Nil. S.A.A. Expended. No E.A.	
"	18/8/17		Fire. Casualties Nil. S.A.A. Expended 5,000 rds. Situation normal. Very heavy shelling by enemy during night. Anti Aircraft report :- Casualties Nil. S.A.A. Expended 1,000 rds. Enemy Aircraft appeared at 9.30 p.m. and dropped bombs in vicinity but were out of range of our guns which opened fire.	

WAR DIARY
INTELLIGENCE SUMMARY.
(Erase heading not required.)

Army Form C. 2118.

Instructions regarding War Diaries and Intelligence Summaries are contained in F.S. Regs., Part II. and the Staff Manual respectively. Title pages will be prepared in manuscript.

19 / 91st Machine Gun Coy.

Place	Date	Hour	Summary of Events and Information	Remarks and references to Appendices
Battle Field	19/8/17		Gen. Casualties Nil. S.A.A. Expended Nil. Situation Normal. Anti-Aircraft report :- S.A.A. Expended Nil. Enemy aeroplanes appeared at 10 p.m. flying high beyond range of our guns.	
"	20/8/17		Wer. Casualties Nil. S.A.A. Expended 4,000 rds. Situation Normal. Enemy shelled our line heavily between the hours of 11 p.m. and 4 a.m. S.A.A. carried to forward dumps aggregated 60,000 rds. Anti-Aircraft Report :- S.A.A. Expended Nil. No enemy aircraft sighted.	
"	21/8/17		Wer. Casualties :- 2 Wounded S.A.A. 2,000 rds. Situation Normal. C.S.M. Rice J.A. and 2/Lt: J. Jenkins M.C. relieved by Lieut. L. Underwood M.C. and Lieut. L.D. James. Anti-Aircraft Report :- S.A.A. Expended Nil. At 9.40 p.m. enemy aircraft dropped bombs on right and left of positions but were out of range of guns. 2/Lt D. Clark reports to Company from base.	
"	22/8/17		Wet and Stormy. Casualties Nil. S.A.A. Expended 23,000 rds on chosen targets. 1,000 rds on enemy aircraft which appeared over Mount Sorrel. The aeroplane was seen to change course and was lighter. Enemy artillery was quiet during the day but increased to the greatest between the hours of 11 p.m. and 4 a.m.	

WAR DIARY
INTELLIGENCE SUMMARY

Army Form C. 2118.

191st Machine Gun Coy

Place	Date	Hour	Summary of Events and Information	Remarks and references to Appendices
In the Field	23/8/17		Stormy. Casualties nil. SAA Expended 10,500 rds. From 12.30 am to 2 am enemy shelled Immouable Trench with gas shells and 5.9 shells. 7 am to 9 am Enemy shelled battery positions with large calibre and minenwerfer gas shells. 2 Aircraft were engaged at 10 am. 1 became unsteady and returned. Anti Aircraft Report. SAA Expended nil. No Enemy aircraft sighted.	
"	24/8/17		Stormy showery. Casualties nil. SAA Expended 24,500 or nearer target. Enemy aircraft were engaged at 7 + 5 pm at about 1,000 ft. Artillery were more unusually quiet until 5 am when all calibres opened out for 40 minutes. 2/Lt H.G.Williamson proceeded on leave to U.K. Anti Aircraft Report – SAA Expended nil. No Enemy aircraft sighted.	
"	25/8/17		Stormy Mist. Casualties nil. SAA Expended nil. Situation normal. Anti Section relief completed at 9.0 am. Hostile artillery was quiet during the day. Anti Aircraft Report – SAA Expended nil. No Enemy Aircraft sighted.	
"	26/8/17		Mist. Casualties nil. SAA Expended nil. Situation normal. Anti Aircraft Report – SAA Expended nil. No Enemy Aircraft sighted.	

Army Form C. 2118.

WAR DIARY
or
INTELLIGENCE SUMMARY. 191st Machine Gun Coy.
(Erase heading not required.)

Place	Date	Hour	Summary of Events and Information	Remarks and references to Appendices
In the field	27/8/17		Stormy. Casualties nil. S.A.A Expended nil. Situation normal.	
			Anti Aircraft Report :- S.A.A Expended nil. No Enemy Aircraft sighted	
"	28/8/17		Showery. Casualties nil. S.A.A Expended nil. Enemy shelling delivered aircraft.	
			increasing in volume for 5 minutes each hour. Emplacements phosgened.	
			Anti Aircraft Report :- S.A.A Expended nil. No Enemy Aircraft sighted	
"	29/8/17		Stormy. Casualties one wounded. S.A.A Expended nil. Situation normal.	
			Intersection relief completed by 9.0 am.	
			Anti Aircraft Report :- S.A.A Expended nil. No Enemy Aircraft sighted	
"	30/8/17		Stormy. Casualties nil. S.A.A Expended nil. Situation normal.	
			Anti Aircraft Report :- S.A.A Expended nil. No Enemy Aircraft sighted	
"	31/8/17		Stormy. Casualties nil. S.A.A Expended nil. Situation normal.	
			Anti Aircraft Report :- S.A.A Expended nil. No Enemy Aircraft sighted	

C.J. Cross Capt.
O.C. 191st Machine Gun Coy

Army Form C. 2118.

WAR DIARY
or
INTELLIGENCE SUMMARY

(Erase heading not required.)

191. M.G. Coy

Vol 10

WAR DIARY
INTELLIGENCE SUMMARY

Army Form C. 2118.

191st Machine Gun Company

Place	Date	Hour	Summary of Events and Information	Remarks and references to Appendices
Hill Fields	1/9/17		Stormy. Company in line S.E. of Ypres. Casualties Nil. S.A.A Expended 3,500 rds on harassing fire. 1,500 rds on Enemy Aircraft. Situation normal. 2 M.G. wounded for Anti-Aircraft duties at Divisional H.Q. report Enemy Aircraft all out of range of guns.	
	2/9/17		Fine. O.C. (Capt. C. J. Cross) leaves for U.K. on appointment to home establishment M.G.T.C. S.A.A. Expended 6,000 rds on alternate shoot bursts on S.O.S. line. Situation normal.	
	3/9/17		Fine. Company in line is relieved by 118th and 228th M.G. Coys. 4.30 p.m. Casualties Nil. S.A.A. Expended on harassing fire 6,000 rds, 2,000 rds on Enemy Aircraft. Situation normal.	
	4/9/17		Fine. 2/Lt. H.G. Williamson returns from leave to U.K. Company in Camp.	
	5/9/17		Fine. Company in Camp.	
	6/9/17		Fine. Henderson 4 Guns and teams detailed for duty against Enemy Aircraft in Zillebeke Lake area under Lieut. L. Anderson M.C. and 2 Lieut. H.G. Williamson. Positions of guns are:- I.22.c.50.80. I.22.d.10.85. (2 guns each)	

Army Form C. 2118.

WAR DIARY
or
INTELLIGENCE SUMMARY.
(Erase heading not required.)

191st Machine Gun Company

Place	Date	Hour	Summary of Events and Information	Remarks and references to Appendices
Battle Field	7/9/17		2 Gun Emplacements constructed at Camps (H.32.c.5.5) for A.A. duties.	
	8/9/17	4 A.M.	H. Teams (2 No 1 - and 2 No 3 Section) proceed to Zillebeke Lake area.	
			Enemy shelling very vigorously our positions near Zillebeke Lake.	
			H. Enemy aircraft passed over our positions about 2.30 pm. Our 2 rear	
			Guns opened fire.	
	9/9/17		3 Officers and 40 O.R. acting as working and carrying party to convey	
			ammunition to dumps for M.G. barrage at Observatory Ridge.	
			5 S.A.A. dumps started between Valley Cottages and Ridden House, consisting	
			of 100,000 rounds each. Situation normal.	
	10/9/17		5 S.A.A. dumps completed. 321,000 rds. carried to forward positions.	
			3 Officers and 50 O.R. of 194 M.G. Coy. are attached to the Company for	
			rations and accommodation. 1 Casualty. Situation normal	
	11/9/17		3 Officers and 24 O.R. (23rd Division) are attached for rations and accommodation.	
			Capt. B. Green arrives at Camps 5.30 pm. and assumes command of Company.	
			Lieut. Morgan P.G. and 9 O.R. relieve 2/Sgt Young E.G. and 9 O.R. on A.A. duty	
			at Divisional H.Q.	

Army Form C. 2118.

WAR DIARY
or
INTELLIGENCE SUMMARY.
(Erase heading not required.)

191st Machine Gun Company

Place	Date	Hour	Summary of Events and Information	Remarks and references to Appendices
Shuttle Field	11/9/17		From O.C. A.A. Battery Zillebeke Lake (Lieut R. Anderson M.C.) During the past 24 hours the enemy has been very active in Zillebeke Lake – Valley Cottage Area. He shelled at intervals with 5.9 and gas shells. At 2 A.M. he brought concentrated fire with gas shells to bear on the above areas. An enemy aircraft passed over Zillebeke Lake at about 5.30 p.m. (10th) at a height of 250 feet. Our guns engaged it and I believe brought it down. He swayed considerably and rode off in the direction of his own line, obviously in difficulties.	
	12/9/17	5 P.M.	Lieut R. Stowe and Lieut G.D. James with teams of Nos. 2 and 4 Sections relieve Lieut R. Anderson M.C. and 2/Lieut. H.G. Williamson with teams of Nos. 1 and 3 Sections at Zillebeke Lake Area.	
		20 P.M.	O.R's proceed to Menin Road vicinity to carry S.A.A. forward to position near Nuckbourn track at about I.24.d.7.4.	
	13/9/17		Fine. Shaking quiet. Forward dumps all now completed. Leaving Camp. Cleaning Limbers, Equipments and sandbagging tents.	
	14/9/17		Fine. 191st M.G. Coy. guns in line are relieved by 94 South Staffs Guns guns 5 P.M	

D. D. & L., London, E.C. (A5853) Wt. W60/M1672 300,000 4/17 Sch. 82a. Forms/C/2118/4

Army Form C. 2118.

WAR DIARY
or
INTELLIGENCE SUMMARY.
191st Machine Gun Company

(Erase heading not required.)

Place	Date	Hour	Summary of Events and Information	Remarks and references to Appendices
In the Field	14/9/17		Lieut. S.H.V. White proceeds on leave to U.K.	
	15/9/17		Guns on A.A. duty at Oriental H.Q. are dismounted and return to camp at 12. Noon. Lieut. A Stone proceeds I/C Advance Party to Herzic Area	
			Company preparing to move	
	16/9/17		Coy. Company parade for inspection 6.30 a.m. Entrain at Hallebast corner 7.0 a.m. Arrive Herzic Area 11.30 a.m. Company H.Q. at Meteren	
	17/9/17		Company resting in billets, Herzic and Meteren Area	
	18/9/17		Company resting in billets, Herzic and Meteren Area 36393 A.C. Denney. P. proceeds on leave to U.K.	
	19/9/17		Company training	
	20/9/17		Company preparing to move. Lieut A Stone I/C advance party proceed by train from Bailleul Station at 9.30 a.m. for Bapaume West.	
	21/9/17		Company parade 11.45 a.m. (approx) and entrain at Bailleul Station. Leave Herzic at 3.31 p.m. Arrive Bapaume 2.30 p.m. Company marches to billets at Ytres arriving 6.0 p.m. 37136 Pte. Cook A. proceeds on leave to U.K. P. 20. 6. (Sheet 57 C)	
	22/9/17		Company resting in billets at Ytres	

WAR DIARY
or
INTELLIGENCE SUMMARY.
(Erase heading not required.)

Army Form C. 2118.

191st Machine Gun Company

Place	Date	Hour	Summary of Events and Information	Remarks and references to Appendices
In the Field	23/9/17		Company fatigues and training.	
	24/9/17		Company training with pack animals. 2 M.G. mounted for A.A. duty at camp. #4733 Pte Ruston T. proceeds on leave to U.K.	
			2 O.R. reinforcement report from A.H.T.D.	
	25/9/17		Company training with pack animals.	
	26/9/17		Company preparing to move. O.C. proceeds to line to arrange taking over positions etc. from 2 Hoth M.G. Coy. Lieut. L. Anderson M.C. works S.O.R.'s proceed to 3rd Army Rest Camp. Lieut Ashurst proceeds i/c Advance party	
	27/9/17		Company parade 9 a.m. March to camp in Mont Allain area north of 17th Inf. Bde. arrive 2.0 p.m. 2/Lt K. Robinson and 2/Lt R. Clark proceed on leave for 14 to Rivieres Lieut L/D James & 2/Lt D. Jenkins reconnoitre positions to be taken over from 2 Hoth M.G. Coy.	
	28/9/17		Company parade 10 a.m. March to Merville. 12 guns proceed to large shelters L. 11. A. 33. at 7 p.m. remainder of Company with H.Q. section proceed to the descent to billets. Transport line at Sterulby Lieut. S.H.V. White returns from leave to U.K.	

WAR DIARY
or
INTELLIGENCE SUMMARY

Army Form C. 2118.

INTELLIGENCE SUMMARY: 190th Machine Gun Company.

Place	Date	Hour	Summary of Events and Information	Remarks and references to Appendices
In the Field	29/9/17		Company (6 sections in reserve) resting in billets. 12 guns barrage laid to drop barrage on line A.26.a.50 to G.8.d.0.0 in answer to S.O.S. the line to include 4 sections I. A.26.a.50 to G.2.a.36. II. G.2.a.36 to G.2.d.58. III. G.2.D.58 to G.8.a.89. IV. G.8.a.89 to G.8.d.00. All 12 guns can switch on to any of these sections. Lieut A. Stone A/Sgt Jannose E.G. A/Cpl Whitehead J, Pte Bacon H. proceed to M.G. Course at Camiers. Cpl Elgar J. returns from M.G. Course. 9 O.R. reinforcement from Base report 10 A.M.	
	30/9/17		5 in Section in reserve, training. O.C. joins company in succ. Pte Carmody returns from leave to U.K. Situation quiet.	

B. Green Capt.
O.C. 190th Machine Gun Company.

"Confidential"

War Diary
of
191 M.G. Coy
for
October 1917

Vol II

191st Machine Gun Company

Army Form C. 2118.

WAR DIARY
INTELLIGENCE SUMMARY
(Erase heading not required.)

October 1917

Place	Date	Hour	Summary of Events and Information	Remarks and references to Appendices
HESBECOURT & LINE	1/10/17	Fine.	2 Sections in line at Barrage position L.11.a.25.70. (Ref. 62c.) Barricade attacks men training at HESBECOURT. 05036 Pte Selmon R. admitted hospital.	
"	2/10/17	Fine.	Lt. D. Clark with 18t Section proceed to HESBECOURT to Barrage position to relieve Lt. A.D. Jones & 2nd Section. Lt. H.C. Villamore resumed command of Barrage Battery vice O.C. who had gone to see M.O.	
"	3/10/17	Fine.	Attacked men proceed to line to replace men transferred to No. 2 Section who are to proceed overseas. 203752/Pte Evans Bh proceed to Omerex & admitted hospital. No 2 Section preparing to proceed to A. Horrie admitted to 20th General hospital whilst attending F.K. Course at CAMIERS.	
"	4/10/17	Fine.		
"	5/10/17	Stormy.	Practice Barrage & concentration role & carried on at 12 Dover Col Barrage. Guns in co-operation with artillery. 9000 do see fired. Tomorro Pte Buston A. & 76. 203745 proceed on leave to U.K.	

WAR DIARY
INTELLIGENCE SUMMARY.
(Erase heading not required.)

Army Form C. 2118.

Place	Date	Hour	Summary of Events and Information	Remarks and references to Appendices
HESBECOURT & LINE.	2/1/17	Army.	2/Lt. R. Clark arrived from leave & is retired to 7/61 T.O. Robinson 7027/1036 L/Cpl. Coys R.E. return from leave. To T.O.T. & trained for overseas with 7th Battalion. 11 o/m. T.O. & Section, consisting of T.O.T. & T. White, 7/61. D. Clark & 303. Athur Ranks, & having been & Whales, & 2 Limbers have Company H.Q. & arrived at 7/61.	
"	3/1/17	Army.	7/61. D. Jenkins T.O. & Cross down line. Lt. W.D. James proceeded to the Scarpe on command of Forage guard from 2/1/17. Lt. G. Williamson, who proceeded to the III Army H.Q. Camps with 2 Men Ranks. 7/8/1/17 the Cavy. 778/1/96 Pte Dodson 676 All took 7/0 Services in course. proceeded on leave to T.O.T. To 258/53 P/ca 10 III Army School of Cookery in course.	
"	4/1/17	Army.	Work carried on as usual.	
"	5/1/17	Army.	Lt. E. Anderson T.O. & 8 other Ranks return from III Army Cookery Comp. 7033/7063 Pte Newton V. Williams from Leave to T.O.T. To 024/6503 Cpl. Rice T.O. & 2/61. Jenkins T.O. & preceded on leave to T.O.T.	

WAR DIARY
INTELLIGENCE SUMMARY
(Erase heading not required.)

Army Form C. 2118.

Place	Date	Hour	Summary of Events and Information	Remarks and references to Appendices
HESBECOURT	10/10/14	Showery.	13,000 rds fired in practice barrage in co-operation with artillery by barrage guns. Company H.Q. etc. to scene killed in ROISEL.	
4 LINE.				
ROISEL	11/10/14	Showery.	Work carried on as usual. 18303193 L/Cpl Tyler L. wounded in line 10.10.6.	
4 LINE	12/10/14	Showery.	Work carried on as usual. 18.08.198 Sgt Bryan R.I. wounded in line 1.16.C.	
"	13/10/14	Showery.	18203819 L/Cpl Case J. wounded with Military Honor killed by explosion III Corps.	
"	14/10/14	Showery.	Two guns teams of No 2 Section withdrawn from 20's to leave killed in ROISEL.	
"	15/10/14	Fine.	10 guns teams in line at barrage position. 18309012 L/Cpl Clayne W.E. proceeds to III Corps school for leave Junior N.C.O.'s course. Practice barrage & concentration defence carried out in co-operation with artillery. S.A.A. expended 12,000 rds.	
"	16/10/14	Fine.	Work carried on as usual.	

WAR DIARY

~~INTELLIGENCE~~ SUMMARY.

(Erase heading not required.)

Army Form C. 2118.

Place	Date	Hour	Summary of Events and Information	Remarks and references to Appendices
ROISEL	17/7/17		Fine. 2 Coys & 1 sec. of 1 Bde Section proceed to Barrage position to relieve 2 other teams of 1 Bde Section.	
LINE	18/7/17		Fine. Work carried on as usual.	
"	19/7/17		Fine. Work carried on as usual. To 3½pm Cpl Williams A. proceeds to Base Depot to purpose of going to GRANTHAM for Special course of instruction.	
"	20/7/17		Fine. 2 Gun teams of 1 Bde Section relieve two gun teams of No 1 Section.	
"	21/7/17		Fine. Work carried on as usual. No 5911 Pte. Lucker G.E. proceeded to PERONNE for Sanitary Course. No 90617 Pte Belsham G admitted to hospital (sick).	
"	22/7/17		Wet. 1767 Cpl. Killingray & S. Mc Carter return from III Army Rest Camp. No 16031 Pte Girard D. proceeds to VRAIGNES for silent signalling course. No 71890 Pte Dunn D. returns to MG return from leave to U.K.	

WAR DIARY
or
INTELLIGENCE SUMMARY

Army Form C. 2118.

Place	Date	Hour	Summary of Events and Information	Remarks and references to Appendices
ROISEL & LINE	23/10/17		_Wet._ 1 Gun team from reserve billet & 2 guns teams from Forage position at L.11.a.05.05 take up position of Coln M.G. Battery at L.17.f.30.25. 2 Bl. Jenkins N.C.O. & 346.93 L/cpl Rice A.C. return with Coln to Fort.	
	24/10/17		_Showery._ 8 Guns & Teams at L.11.a.05.30. & 3 guns & teams at L.17.f.30.25. 2 Lt. H.A. Williamson & 2/Lt. D. Perkins M.C. relieve 2/Lt. L.D. James & 2/Lt. H.C. Robinson. 34/683 Cpl Rice N. goes to Forage position. 2/Lt. Raymond takes over command of Forage Guns. No. 81111 Pte Perry f. Wilson from leave to Fort. No. 083141 Cpl Fairy G. Thomas on leave to Fort.	
	23/10/17		_Stormy._ 18 Guns & Teams at L.11.a.05.30. & 3 guns & teams at L.17.f.30.25. No. 92602 L/Cpl Pritchard H. & Gunner Hope First Earnest on leave to Fort. No. 76511 Pte Sickels 65 returned from service.	
	26/10/17		_Fine._ Work carried on as usual.	

WAR DIARY

INTELLIGENCE SUMMARY
(Erase heading not required.)

Army Form C. 2118.

Place	Date	Hour	Summary of Events and Information	Remarks and references to Appendices
ROISEL Y-LINE	27/10/17		Fine. 100870/y 5156 Sewing (?) A/L 253767/c Carrell to admitted hospital (sick) 08568/Cpl Chip Wellmore being attached to our Reinforce Coy. 104019 & Cpl Ayler C. & L/C 46119 L/Cpl Hayer G.L. returned of the leave to U.K. L/Cpl 78570 L/Cpl Cook H. returned from Cooker course.	
"	28/10/17		Wet. 107209 L/Cpl Jenkins C. arrives from base depot as relief. 107611 L/Cpl Custer C.C. proceeds to Sanctuary (overseas?) (overstrength). I am seen of No 1 Section relieves I am seen of same section.	
"	29/10/17		Showery. 25038 Cpl Tolys ? proceeds to Embrance debot Shaftoff ? children hospital (sick)	
"	30/10/17		Wet. Unit carried on as usual.	
"	31/10/17		Fine. Unit carried on as usual.	

NSGreen Captain
O.C. 191st Machine Gun Company

WAR DIARY.
191st MACHINE GUN COMPANY.
From Nov 1st To Nov 30th
1917

SECRET

Original.

WAR DIARY
or
INTELLIGENCE SUMMARY.

Place	Date	Hour	Summary of Events and Information	Remarks and references to Appendices
POTSEL.	1/11/17		Fine. 11 Guns teams in line. 1 Gun team of 1st Section at Wishtoep #5088. The Bugnes. 1 Offrs.'s detail to proceed to V.H. Corps School to Oufflay. Corpl. S.'5'22. McPherson E.'76 admitted hospital. Gun team of 1st section in 1st relief. Another team of same section #2004 by Lorrell A attached to 11 Gun Bde (8th Royal Inst. Kent) for two weeks.	
Morey.	2/11/17		2/Lt. H.C. Egan & 2/Lt. R. Keirby rejoin from Bde. Rest are taken Tupley. 3/1923 L/Cpl Warneford returns from furlough 6.6. to Bruce. Recreation room in operation with artillery cellar 7.1. Commencing 2.2.31 Cm. S.R.d. Expenden 80.00 rad.	
Morey.	3/11/17		1 Gun team of 157th section relieve 1 Gun team of 151st section. 1611 L/Cpl Licker 6.6. returns from Sanitary Corps. 0303'4 Cpl. Bryan (W) returns from Gas Course.	

Army Form C. 2118.

WAR DIARY
~~INTELLIGENCE SUMMARY~~
(Erase heading not required.)

Army Form C. 2118.

Place	Date	Hour	Summary of Events and Information	Remarks and references to Appendices
ROISEL	31/11/17	(cont)	No 2 & 3 & 4 Pl the English & The Queens attached proceed on leave to N.Z.	
"	1/12/17	Showery	16.11.0/17 Pte Shelton to admitted hospital. 0/11/05 Pte Gowan R. proceeds on leave to N.Z.	
"	2/12/17	Showery	10-28002 Pte Everett C. returns from hospital. Gun team of No 2 section relieved Gun team of same section.	
"	3/12/17	Showery	10-2807 Pte Sutton C returns from hospital. Gun team of No 1 section relieves Gun team of No 3 section. 10 20416 L/Cpl Tonnie to proceeds to E.O. class GNRS. 2/Lt G.E. Wilkinson resumes command of Barrage Guns on 2/Lt G.R. James ceasing to be O/c N.Z.	
"	4/12/17	Fine	Nil of cause of no count.	
"	5/12/17	Fine	2/Lt G.R. James resumes duties of Second in Command vice Lt. McKerron.	

WAR DIARY / INTELLIGENCE SUMMARY

Army Form C. 2118.

Place	Date	Hour	Summary of Events and Information	Remarks and references to Appendices
POPSEL	10/11/17	Showery	1 Gun team of No 3 Section relieved 1/1 Gun team of same section from Rest Billet. Hostile bombing planes coming over line. Consolidation scheme carried out in cooperation with artillery. S.O.S. Expended 19,000 rds. Ø506z The Kemmelberg. No service on line to H.Q. 58564 The Kusttbl Klemper. F. H.Q. lad & truck of ration.	
	11/11/17	Showery	Col. Robinson visited on the works. Spare one to H.Q. Hostile aeroplane shelling near Company depot at Ras depot. Hobrot Pe Aulne of Annelles hospital. Harassing fire carried out during night. Ldr. Expended 16,000 rds.	
	12/11/17	Fine	F.58.067 Yph Fishey Gn return from hospital. Ø.05.119 off Fir L.W. proceed to En Rouse. F.76.11.66 Lucker C6. proceed to take duty Cont. 1 sec of 8th Buffs (to Feale) relief 10.16 Nielsen vice them of 1st B.L. Ø5602 Pe Kanely of Annelles hospital.	

WAR DIARY
INTELLIGENCE SUMMARY
(Erase heading not required.)

Army Form C. 2118.

Place	Date	Hour	Summary of Events and Information	Remarks and references to Appendices
ROISEL	3/1/14	Fine/Fine	1 Gun team of No 3 Section relieve 1 Gun team of No 1 Section. 70022541 Cpl Waring G. 9802 L/Cpl Gilchrist W.J. & 17277 Pte Evans T return from leave to M.G.C. 17777.25 Pte McDonald R. admitted hospital.	
"	14/1/14	Fine	4 Men of No 1 B.T.F. return to Battalion. 4 Men of 8th Buffs forward to line. 054038 Pte Entwich T. admitted hospital. 286735 Pte Willans A.H. proceeds on leave to U.K. 283398 Pte Belladine F. proceeds to Corps Rest camp.	
"	15/1/14	Fine	1 Gun team of No 1 Section relieves 1 Gun team of No 3 Section. W/L/Cpl Dangerfield reports from Base Dept. on duty. No transport officer. 16811 Pte Tucker S.S. returns from U.K. on duty leave.	
"	16/1/14	Fine	See letter at L.H.C. L.G. pneumonia now is remaining Trench army. Lt. Fred. Williamson comes North line to Coy. H.Q.	

Army Form C. 2118.

WAR DIARY
or
INTELLIGENCE SUMMARY.
(Erase heading not required.)

Instructions regarding War Diaries and Intelligence Summaries are contained in F.S. Regs., Part II. and the Staff Manual respectively. Title pages will be prepared in manuscript.

Place	Date	Hour	Summary of Events and Information	Remarks and references to Appendices
RYVEL.	17/11/17		Fine. Pte. W.P. Bengel, the Munroe line Pte. H.E. R.A. Williamson. 6080+ Pte. Sutton C. 3.2002 Pte. Ramsey T. 47003S-Pte. McBride D. Transferred to 1/5 West Surrey Rt Strength.	
"	18/11/17		Fine. 038388 Cpl Jackson T.G. proceeds to Base depot for purpose of going to GRANTHAM on course of instruction. 37 9043 Sgt. Grey J. proceeds on leave to U.K. 47039 Sgt. Harwood A. rejoins Company after being attached 1/7am Inf. Bde.	
"	19/11/17		Fine. 280539 Cpl Ballyrell proceeds on leave to U.K. 37940 Cpl. Shipland R. proceeds to En Course at VII Corps Checkout.	
"	20/11/17		Dull Wet. At 6.20am our fire was opened onl in accordance with Divisional orders. Shortly after commencement enemy sent up many colored lights. But no retaliation took place. S.A.A. expended. By Coppns. Very quiet during reminder of day & night.	
"	21/11/17		Dull Wet. 407 290317 Pte. Hepton (Lt. Revers, attached) relieved from leave to U.K.	

A6945. Wt. W14122/M1160 350,000 12/16 D.D.& L. Forms/C./2118/14.

WAR DIARY
or
INTELLIGENCE SUMMARY.

Army Form C. 2118.

Place	Date	Hour	Summary of Events and Information	Remarks and references to Appendices
ROISEL	22/11/18		Snr. Work carried on as usual.	
	23/11/18		1st Bn. At 5:15am 6:05am guns opened fire (11.a.35.30) in co-operation with Artillery. Enemy retaliated 5:05am to 5:55am on HARICOURT 6:05am on HARICOURT in vicinity of Sunken road at L.H.C.Y.H. Total number of rounds fired 18,000. Enna at L.I.4. F.28.30 fired from 5:12am until 5:15am 9pm 6:52am to 6:56am. No of rounds fired not known. Enemy retaliated by searching ridge near gun positions with 5.9" H.E. shells. Signal always with 96th Queens when enemy attempted to leave behind German lines, e.g. Very lights fired 17 times on positions.	
	24/11/18		Drill as ahead. 3rd Bn Lpl Whitehead W. returned from line Car vet. Harassing fire carried out on tracks & roads behind enemy line. S.A.A. Expended 15,000 rds. 24/11/18 S.A.A. Expended 15,000 rds. 24/11/18 [illegible] The Drinoille of Provence on leave 18/6/16	

Army Form C. 2118.

WAR DIARY
or
INTELLIGENCE SUMMARY
(Erase heading not required.)

Place	Date	Hour	Summary of Events and Information	Remarks and references to Appendices
ROISEL.	26/11/17		Showery. Harassing fire carried out on Macke Kopje line enemy's line from 6pm to 6.30am. 2/Lt Spencer 20,378 Rds. 2/11/03 2/Lt Brian B. returned from leave. 38,138 Rds. Enemy's return from hospital.	
	26/11/17		November. Harassing fire carried out 8 p.m. 25/11/17 to 6 a.m. 26/11/17. 2/Lt. Spencer 25,000 rds. 2/Lt D. Jenkins T.C. 30,938 rds. Major R. L. Vowdry Holland (officers course) Reports to VII Corps Andershot. Relieve arrive. 2/Lt H.O.G. Williamson goes to line to/vice 2/Lt. D. Jenkins T.C. 2/Lt. G.B. Fane goes to line of takes over command of courage gun from 2/Lt. to Andrew T.C. who takes charge of Livery Room.	
	27/11/17		Fine.	
	28/11/17		Fine. T/63862 Gr. Cummings J.C. return from leave to T.O.B. T/63233 Gr. Ormway T. & T/17753 Gr. Thomas A.E. admitted.	

WAR DIARY or INTELLIGENCE SUMMARY

Army Form C. 2118.

Place	Date	Hour	Summary of Events and Information	Remarks and references to Appendices
ROMSEL.	29/11/17	Fine.	10.031 The Bulk of Returns from Signalling course. H.Q. 2nd Lt Williamson v 2/Lt 6.A. Pic Calpin C.E. McEvoy R. (Can.) joined. 10 MAJT ALLAINES no further party to arrange billets &c in Entrenent which is to move the Bn.	
	30/11/17	Fine.	All news to move me cancelled. operation line to take command of own. Bon stood to complete attached to 47th Infly. Arrangements made with Division. Signals as to cover to be taken in case of attack by enemy. All details in ROMSEL "stand to" are in readiness to act as reserve to Officer i/c ROMSEL defences in the event of enemy breaking through our lines. Heavy fire carried out on lines Truckies behind enemy's lines night of 29/30th. S.A.A. expended. forward.	Bigger Left OC 141-MG Coy

A6945 Wt. W14422/M1160 350,000 12/16 D. D. & I. Forms/C./2118/74

Original 1/101st Machine Gun Company

WAR DIARY
or
INTELLIGENCE SUMMARY
(Erase heading not required.)

Army Form C. 2118.

December 1917.

Vol 13

Place	Date	Hour	Summary of Events and Information	Remarks and references to Appendices
POTIJZE	12/12/17	Fine	2/Lt H.G. Williamson, Pte Parkin & Hedley return from leave. 2/Lt H.G. Parkin not cancelled. 7Pte I.P. Parkin offc. 307298 L/Cpl Morgan J.G., 307207 Pte Bullock G. (Mess dressers) return from III Corps Gas School & Escort Coy line. 373373- Pte Bullows J.B. returns from leave to H.Q. 6 guns at "Savage" positions at BUFFS QUARRY. 2 guns at CAUTION DUGOUT & two others & two others 6.32am. 21 May TEMPLEUX. Hostile artillery fairly quiet until 6.32am. 21 May.	
21/12/17		Fine	rifle fire was at the Irish shelling of L.14.b. 7d.5. (CAUTION PADDOCK). Enemy shelled support about 50 yards in front of guns at L.14.b. 35.70. with light H.E. shells. S.A.A.Expended 17rds. 10.125. Reynolds Ernest 40850 line fires transferred lives to take charge of transfered section.	
30/12/17		Fine	1919 Pte McBee F. (1st Yorks Lt. Wheeler) received on leave to 76.6. 15119 Cpl Hart G.L. proceeds to III Corps Infantry School up course. Enemy shells rifle in front of CAUTION DUGOUT with H.E. shells.	
31/12/17		Fine	1700 responded on S.O.S. Target 4 guns at CAUTION DUGOUT to prevent water freezing in breech.	

A6945. Wt. W1142/M1160. 350,000 12/16 D.D.&L. Forms/C./2118/14.

WAR DIARY
or
INTELLIGENCE SUMMARY

Army Form C. 2118.

Place	Date	Hour	Summary of Events and Information	Remarks and references to Appendices
ANSEL	25/9/17	Cont.	Harassing fire carried out all night at CAUTION DUGOUT. S.A.A. expended 1000 rds. 8.30pm O.C. Garrison 6/34 D.LI. reported from A.N.T.D. Sgt. Porter 10 Shropshire Light Infantry to Mines. 9.30pm Bde Commr O.C. Garrison on line 1/1.L.I. 11.0 am Inspection of Garrison Battery Trench. Junction 2/4. Busby Quarry & Junction Enemy Battery Trench. Junction 27J. BUSBY QUARRY & CAUTION DUGOUT as usual.	
✓	26/9/17	Cont.	Harassing fire carried out during night. S.A.A. expended. BUSBY QUARRY - 300 rds. CAUTION DUGOUT - 1,100 rds. Enemy placed in vicinity of CAUTION DUGOUT & the shell entered trench used fire to 5 rifles S.A.A.	
✓	27/9/17	Cont.	Harassing fire carried out in the enemy trenches rear of KID LANE & KID TRENCH. S.A.A. expended: BUSBY QUARRY - 1300 rds. CAUTION DUGOUT - 430 rds. 3.30pm Lt. Burke (458.053) 1/Bn D.L.I. & 2/Lt. G. Anderson M.C. 2/3 D.L.I. & 2/Lt. J.F. Winnacombe return from leave 10/M.R.C. 8/9.29 2/Lt. Baldwin J. & 803yl Bde Signaller J. (Officers of) Proceed I.B.D. G. Corner at CAMIERS.	

Army Form C. 2118.

WAR DIARY
or
INTELLIGENCE SUMMARY.
(Erase heading not required.)

Instructions regarding War Diaries and Intelligence Summaries are contained in F. S. Regs., Part II. and the Staff Manual respectively. Title pages will be prepared in manuscript.

Place	Date	Hour	Summary of Events and Information	Remarks and references to Appendices
RASEN.	9/12/17	Thurs.	Evening fire carried out by Pros at CAUTION DUGOUT. S.A.A. expended 50 rds.	
	9/12/17	Thurs.	20.10 Pe Atkins 27487931 Rifle Bde to admitted hospital. 5.A.A. expended at CAUTION DUGOUT 2570 rds. 27/931 Rifle Bde 6	
	10/12/17	Thurs.	discharged from hospital. S.A.A. expended at CAUTION DUGOUT 2054 rds.	
	11/12/17	Tues.	10.10 pm expense by Pro at CAUTION DUGOUT. 2752-62 Pe Edw. Rif. moved on June to Ket.	
	12/12/17	Wed.	1530 rds expended by Pros at CAUTION DUGOUT.	
	13/12/17	Thurs.	1530 rds S.A.A. expended by Pros at CAUTION DUGOUT. 1082233-Pe Slater G.C. admitted hospital. 24901 Pe Prentice S. returned from care to Ket. 20 Pe Gr. Spencer returned from care to Ket.	
	14/12/17	Fri.	12651 Pe Bush T. (Shoffs attacked) returned from care to Ket.	
	15/12/17	Sat.	10802396 Slater G.R. 276 returned from hospital. 1500 rds S.A.A. expended by Pros at CAUTION DUGOUT. 25039 Pe Kingers. proceed to Harris A.E.	
	16/12/17	Sun.	10.30 pm Cpl. Gohin L. admitted hospital. 2/Lt. O. Kinley 10200 Pe Harris A.E. 9 Lieut Pe Walker B. arrive from Base Depot	

WAR DIARY
INTELLIGENCE SUMMARY
(Erase heading not required.)

Army Form C. 2118.

Place	Date	Hour	Summary of Events and Information	Remarks and references to Appendices
RUYSEL	16/2/17	Noon	2/Lt. H.A.Williamson proceeds on leave to U.K. 11950 Pte Summerfield W. admitted hospital. 25995 Pte George Caldwillie hospital S.A.A. expended 450 rds	
	17/2/17	Noon	4300 rds S.A.A. expended by guns at CAUTION DUGOUT. 23798 Pte Thorpe W. admitted hospital.	
	18/2/17	Noon	5790 rds S.A.A. expended by guns at CAUTION DUGOUT. 23/184 Sgt. [illegible] on leave to U.K. 38834 Cpl Bally S.E. admitted hospital	
	19/2/17	Noon	S.A.A. expended by guns at CAUTION DUGOUT 15-rounds. Enemy seen in vicinity of BOBBY QUARRY during day. 38505-J Cpl [illegible] evacuated to No.55 Fd & Luck of Sheppk. Cpl [illegible] proceeds on leave to PARIS.	
	2/2/17	Noon	2000 rds expended by guns at CAUTION DUGOUT. 2/Lt. J.Kimber takes over Command of guns at CAUTION DUGOUT from 2/Lt H.G.Pelman who proceeds to passage positions at BOBBY QUARRY. 160335- Pte Slater C.H. admitted hospital.	

Army Form C. 2118.

WAR DIARY
or
INTELLIGENCE SUMMARY.
(Erase heading not required.)

Place	Date	Hour	Summary of Events and Information	Remarks and references to Appendices
ROISEL	21/12/17	12 noon	15/DLI relieved 1/5 gords at CAUTION DUGOUT, 2 pins at CAUTION DUGOUT relieved by 2 pins of Cavalry M.G. Squadron 76d. D Limber Gunners to BOSSY QUARRY & 2/6 R.B. Carriers with 3 pins teams from CAUTION DUGOUT came to ROISEL. 4082 Pte Hope Mitchell R.E. admitted hospital.	
✓	22/12/17	12pd	1 Pm team at TEMPLEUX relieved by 2/6 R.B. relieved by River to ROISEL. 119pd Pte Summerfield relieved by 48602 Pte Hope. Bridges recce to TOOLE & 1055 *8d* relieved by Sheyth.	
✓	23/12/17	12pd	08402 Pte Ardmore a.s. returned from leave 16/6 7/6. F. A. Gordon report from Base Depot.	
✓	24/12/17	9pm	4919 Pte McDuff (as H. Staff) returns from leave 10/6/16.	
✓	25/12/17	Thurs.	1st Company Walmer Christmas Dinner served.	
✓	26/12/17	Thurs.	2nd Company in line relieved Walmer Christmas Dinner	
			by those who were present Christmas Day.	
✓	26/12/17	12pd	Ink carrier ill as usual.	
✓	27/12/17	12pd	Cpl B. Green returns from Paris. 08038 Pte Gwerry returns	

Army Form C. 2118.

WAR DIARY
or
INTELLIGENCE SUMMARY.
(Erase heading not required.)

Instructions regarding War Diaries and Intelligence Summaries are contained in F. S. Regs., Part II. and the Staff Manual respectively. Title pages will be prepared in manuscript.

Place	Date	Hour	Summary of Events and Information	Remarks and references to Appendices
RUSEL	28/12/1 (contd)		from Hospital. S.H. attended of 1170 wa. 5.9.110 of Cpl Goodwin S.	
"	29/12/1		First. Grenades on issue 1 lot.	
			291. D. Jenkins R.E. M.O.19. Cpl Wardle a. 1040314 attached.	
			(Officer Oty.) Moved Tallana Camp at 5th Army Infantry School	
"	30/12/1		Obser. New section arrived consisting of Lt. C. B. Harris, L/Sgt M.S.F	
			Burns, 25-OR, 11 horses, 2 limbers & 2 gims.	
"	31/12/1		Noth. S.A. attended 10,000 ws. 6,000 ws fired on backs position	
			Enemy's line infantry in front lines having been considerable	
			movement at dusk & dawn.	
				B. Coy — Brit
				86.19.91 Machine Gun Coy

191st Machine Gun Company

Original

WAR DIARY
INTELLIGENCE SUMMARY
(Erase heading not required.)

Army Form C. 2118.

Place	Date	Hour	Summary of Events and Information	Remarks and references to Appendices
RYSSEL	1/1/18	Ord.	6 Guns at Barrage position BUSBY QUARRY. 15,000 rds S.A.A. expended on Enemy's behind enemy's lines. 4 Guns on A.A. duty at RYSSEL. 6 in reserve. 10/10 Get Harrold R.A. admitted hospital. 37742 Pte Earle 27th (R.I.Rifles) proceeds on one month's furlough. Pte Thomas & Pte Wainwright hospital. 22310 Pte Curry furlough.	
"	2/1/18	Ord.	10 K.H. Stationary Camps & Sheets of Sheep. 10,000 rds S.A.A. expended by guns at BUSBY QUARRY on enemy's behind enemy's lines. 20339 Pte Lavish admitted to American hospital.	
"	3/1/18	Gen.	6,000 rds S.A.A. expended by guns at BUSBY QUARRY on targets behind enemy's lines. 11/203 Pte Cleary admitted hospital. 9 353-30 Pte Gibbs L/Cl. 56050 L/Cpl Barnett 105 L/Cpl Chappel sent on leave to UK.	
"	4/1/18	Ord.	6,000 rds S.A.A. expended by guns at BUSBY QUARRY on targets behind enemy's lines.	
"	5/1/18	Ord.	Targets engaged by guns at BUSBY QUARRY. 11485 Released Cpl. Hayes & 130216 Pte McKinney & 4304 Pte Allen L/Cpl & 130216 Pte McKinney admitted hospital.	

WAR DIARY
or
INTELLIGENCE SUMMARY

Army Form C. 2118.

191st MACHINE GUN COMPANY.

Place	Date	Hour	Summary of Events and Information	Remarks and references to Appendices
POSEL	3/11/18		08.40H The Coys L 23.95, the Recoof & 192 the Enemy of [illegible] moved to HQrs 09.03H 54 Guns L returning from line to HQrs.	
POSEL	4/11/18		Fine. Barrage guns fired at intervals during night on targets behind enemy's line. Stationary Guns EA Vens on the lines & Number of Shots on POSEL. 07.30H 183/54 Coys fir. 08.30H Both Coys & 238/54 Eight Machine Gunners on leave 09.30H with Lieut F.D. Pett [illegible] Col McLellan J.F. Morris (Ret) 10.30H with Lieut FO Arthur[illegible] 13.30H Sergt Whiteway to H.Q. came to HQrs. [illegible] (officers dressed) driven 07.9.19 Col Dickson & 163/54 the Sergeant [illegible] on M.G. Course at Camiers.	
POSEL	5/11/18		Fine. [illegible] Hostile & Stationary M.G. guns at POSEL Carry 08570 the Coys L.F. 3438? the Shoot B 08028 the Entire J. Jones the Lorbe [illegible] moved on leave to HQrs 08.30 the Bugle Band & Col [illegible] on leave to HQrs 2 guns [illegible] proceed [illegible] Div for F.A. duty.	

Army Form C. 2118.

WAR DIARY
or
INTELLIGENCE SUMMARY.

(Erase heading not required.)

191st MACHINE GUN COMPANY.

No ....
Date ....

Instructions regarding War Diaries and Intelligence Summaries are contained in F. S. Regs., Part II. and the Staff Manual respectively. Title pages will be prepared in manuscript.

Place	Date	Hour	Summary of Events and Information	Remarks and references to Appendices
Ronssoy	8/1/18	First	6.00 am referred 1/pers at Bosy QUARRY 12018 OCCURRED	
			Fitted to coverse at 5th Army School at Dernaut high Ocurrered	
			7.45 am OC Storn am 10.45 am OC Major more OC strip	
			Fired 1 supplying norm and 5th Dirin Lignalling school	
			12.15 OC Ellore R. E. (Rhon) attacked somewhere reconnoitred	
	9/1/18	Snowstorm.		
			2.30 am S.A.A. referred 1/prs at Bosy QUARRY 37/23.15	
			Redman R. Warten on leave toth	
	10/1/18	Snowstorm	4.30 am S.A.A. referred 1/prs at Bosy QUARRY on	
			Loyed behind enemy lines 36/... OC Helton & Herrin	
			on leave toth	
	11/1/18	Fine	6.30 am S.A.A. referred 1/pers at Bosy QUARRY	
			Lt. C. Andersson N.o. 5359/ Sgt. Osmchen Joined on leave	
			toth	
	12/1/18	Fine	6.00 am referred 1/pers at Bosy QUARRY 37/29 Cpl.	
			Wilkin J. Warten on leave toth	

WAR DIARY
or
INTELLIGENCE SUMMARY

(Erase heading not required.)

Army Form C. 2118.

191st MACHINE GUN COMPANY.

No. ....
Date ....

Instructions regarding War Diaries and Intelligence Summaries are contained in F. S. Regs., Part II. and the Staff Manual respectively. Title pages will be prepared in manuscript.

Place	Date	Hour	Summary of Events and Information	Remarks and references to Appendices
ROISEL	13/11/8		Fus. 6.750 m S.A.A. expended 161 guns at BUSSY QUARRY 055729. The N.E.C.O. R. 2183/1 The Reform covered in front 1426.	
"	14/11/8		Fus. 8.700 m S.A.A. expended 137 guns at BUSSY QUARRY 38576. The Contain E.O. pioneers on leave 11.11.16. 129th Epl. Lewing B pioneers on S.O. pioneers are leave 11.11.16. Cpl. Coles absent.	
"	15/11/8		Fusilain. 6.750 m Tired 137 guns at BUSSY QUARRY 05819. Fus. N.T. 7 07595 Seminar leave on leave 11.11.16	
"	16/11/8		Fus. 2000 m expended. N.C.O.s at BUSSY QUARRY 041 the. Handley & Stephen & Robinson & Johnson for ordinary 91. E.O. men at 9440 Cpl Fuhler W & 03637 Feltham & Cpt. pioneers on leave 11.11.16	
"	17/11/8		Fuch. 1120 m S.A.A. fired 131 guns at BUSSY QUARRY 033629 2/Cpl. Cope S. N.I.W. 055769 Pte Wicks W.I. + 38745 Pte Line H pioneers on leave 11.11.16	
"	18/11/8		Cold. Work carried on as usual. 38740 2/Cpl Fearning Geo. surveyed to Hants. while duty covered	

WAR DIARY or INTELLIGENCE SUMMARY

Army Form C. 2118.

191st MACHINE GUN COMPANY.

Place	Date	Hour	Summary of Events and Information	Remarks and references to Appendices
RUSSEL	19/1/18		Rain. 37/030 L/Cpl Hague L.E., 53345 Pte Alchin E.J. 93585? to/ftr were E. Pioneers on leave N.E. 31405/ftr Lceporal W.J. returned from N.Bse Ord: Corps. 35030 to/Cpl Cook H. & 038430 A/Cpl Chorbel. return from leave to N.E.	
	20/1/18		Fine. Arms et Orders. Rifles during rain 15/1/18 N.Bgles.	
			S.A.A. Expended 10/5/18 rds. May 18 & May 16 & 15470 Pte Bunbaugh S.	
			Proceed on leave L-N.E.	
	21/1/18		Rain. 35030 Pte Pitt W.E. return from leave to N.E. 34403 Pte Bray E.	
			Admitted Hospital. 27/931 L/Cpl leave to 1.Bse Pte Penny G.	
			37060 Pte Townsend J.E. Procced on leave N.E.	
	22/1/18		Rain. 37070 Lce Sgt Atkinson to Francs for Lee N.E. 05054	
			L/Cpl Evans J.A. 35630 Pte Bond R. & 008700 L/Cpl Harlow E.	
			return from leave N.E.	
	23/1/18		Fire. Fire called out on Enemys lines, felin Enemys lines S.R.Expended 2900 r. 35076 Pte Henry W.F. 35339 Pte Owen E. 3601 Pte Carter F. 12003	
			Pte Price A.E. (Pte Paul Collected) return from leave to N.E. 30440 Pte	
			(Illegible) Proceed on leave N.E.	

WAR DIARY or INTELLIGENCE SUMMARY

Army Form C. 2118.

191ST MACHINE GUN COMPANY.

Place	Date	Hour	Summary of Events and Information	Remarks and references to Appendices
ROSEL	24/1/18		Fine. S.A.A. Expended 12 guns at 8083 Y QUARRY. 2000 rds. 761 S/Kinder proceeds to Wissers Corner on Machine Gun Instruction in Divisional Reserve. 053385. L/Cpl Carr E. 483865 Pte Dixon R.B. proceed on leave to U.K. 033170. L/Cpl Saunders R.D. returns from leave to U.K. 31190 Pte Field J. admitted to hospital. Influenza. 1. 85th Scot. Rifles.	
	25/1/18	Midnight	Fine. Enemy fire carried out on unseen work. Nil in enemy's wire. S.A.A. Expended 3,000 rds. 35447 L/Cpl Featherby A. & 283181 Pte Turner R.B. proceed on leave to U.K. 305542 Pte Faber O. returns from leave to U.K. 38139 L/M/Cough wounded Influenza.	
	26/1/18		Fine. 761 S/Kinder returns from course. 38691 L/Cpl Gibbin S.E. returns from leave to U.K. 056916 Pte Evans A. joins Cpl. Rea A. 08208 Pte Curtis I. proceed on leave to U.K. Guns at 8083 Y QUARRY fire on See Arrangements Form 1318. Night Fullilove S.A.A. Expended 3000 rds.	

WAR DIARY or INTELLIGENCE SUMMARY

Army Form C. 2118.

191st MACHINE GUN COMPANY.

Place	Date	Hour	Summary of Events and Information	Remarks and references to Appendices
ROYSEL	28/11/16		Fine. Morning expended 151 rounds of S.A.A. on QUARRY. 0730 1st Div Bn L/Cpl 028595 Pte Beach L.G. & 26193 Pte Quinn L proceed on leave to U.K. 1230 L/Cpl 123346 Pte Hering L admitted to hospital.	
	29/11/16		Fine. 0700 hrs S.A.A. expended 151 rounds. 0900 hrs 38398 Pte Ballantine J returned from leave to U.K. 1/Lt McCormick proceeds on leave to U.K. 1025/6 Pte Hering L transferred to 16o'b hospital.	
			& Lieut. of Bright A.A. gun at Brinvilliers returns from to Royse.	
	29/11/16		Fine. 1000 hrs expended 151 Large Ammn. L.G. flying low over Royse. night 151 R.L.G.A. Towards HERVILLY. Gun fires of serum etc. hostile out of range. S.A.A. expended 600 rds. Lt. Van Stapler proceeds to MONTIGNY FARM. 019/4 Pte Alexander Ed, 026713 Pte Gummers H. 2084/09 Pte Godwin A, 02639 Pte Graven W, 023739 Pte Webb C, 1631/1 Pte Ferguson L, 023536 Pte Larson H.6. Winkler from leave to U.K.	
	30/11/16		Fine. Harassing fire carried out 151 Large Ammn. S.A.A. expended 1,032 rds. 023574 Pte Webb Bingham B, 023569 Pte & Sgt Bristol L, 2803/41 Pte Hoye L proceed 1045/16 1st Bn & approx 11th Army from leave to Training Corps.	

WAR DIARY
INTELLIGENCE SUMMARY

Army Form C. 2118.

Place	Date	Hour	Summary of Events and Information	Remarks and references to Appendices
Romsen	27/1/18		Line. Harassing fire carried out by Barrage from Stk. Eyhence Londres 33951 Pt sheared W pivoting on line to Pts. 33919 Pt fired N. of, 23.3.925. Pt single @ 443348. Pt relieve opn leave to Pts.	

13 Sept Loft
[signature]
O.C. 191st Machine Gun Company

191st Machine Gun Coy.
Vol 5
Army Form C. 2118.

WAR DIARY
INTELLIGENCE SUMMARY.
(Erase heading not required.)

February 1918.

Place	Date	Hour	Summary of Events and Information	Remarks and references to Appendices
ROISEL	1/2/18	Fine	8 guns at L.11.a.35.30 (BOBBY QUARRY), 2 guns in ROISEL on AA duty. 2 guns at NOBESCOURT FARM on AA Duty. 4 guns at Company HQ. ROISEL in reserve. 15,000 rds expended by guns at BOBBY QUARRY 58388 Pte Bradley G proceeds on leave to UK.	
	2/2/18	Fine	2500 rds expended by guns at BOBBY QUARRY. 2 AA guns at ROISEL relieved by 2 guns of 73rd MG Coy. 4 guns of N°1 Section relieve 4 guns of 73rd MG Coy at F.26.d.7.3. (HEMPLEUX CEMETERY) 58103 Pte Guilbourn G.+ 58574 Pte Hanby proceed on leave to UK. Lt G. D. James L.+ Anderson A.I.C. return from leave to UK. 129966 Pte Lucas admitted to hospital wounded. 133180 Pte Brown AA returns from cookery Course.	
	3/2/18	Fine	2000 rds expended by guns at BOBBY QUARRY. 219135 Sgt. Rouse J. proceeds to attend course at Army Signal School DUNSTABLE ENGLAND, + so struck off strength. 2 Lt Y Algordon proceeds on leave to UK. 5580 Pte Rootes PA (9th R. Irish attached) proceeds to his Battalion to make preparations for leave to UK. 2 Lt H. Jenkins MG 142039 Sgt Woodall R + 54501 Pte __ return from Infantry School. 59410 Pte 142039 Sgt Whitehead VS 37634 Pte Parkin EN 58769 Pte Wiseko WA + 36 mls Pte Rice G return from leave to UK.	
	4/2/18	Fine	Barrage guns fire at intervals during night SAA Expended 2000 rds. Pte Turner J.C. proceeds on leave to UK. 133889 C/Sgt Lockin Y. min return from leave to UK. Lt G.D. James takes over command of barrage guns from BSM Harris + 2 Lt Murry Brown comes down line.	
	5/2/18	Fine	Enemy artillery exceptionally heavy in vicinity + forward of BOBBY QUARRY. At 10 pm 4/2/18 enemy commences to shell our front line again at 10:30 pm our artillery opened out in reply. Bombardment continues with growing intensity until 10:45 pm when it became very heavy. Although no SOS signals were observed our barrage battery at BOBBY QUARRY "closes" to our	

WAR DIARY
or
INTELLIGENCE SUMMARY
(Erase heading not required.)

Army Form C. 2118.

Instructions regarding War Diaries and Intelligence Summaries are contained in F. S. Regs., Part II. and the Staff Manual respectively. Title pages will be prepared in manuscript.

Place	Date	Hour	Summary of Events and Information	Remarks and references to Appendices
Roclin court	2/2/18	contd	Slow fire was opened along barrage lines as a precautionary measure. Bombardment continued to hot heavy until 11.15pm after which it died down quickly. At 11.20pm "Cease fire" was given and at 11.45pm from the battery "stand down" against. BOMBY QUARRY and vicinity were shelled on & off receiving part of the night & again heavily from 6am to 6.30am. S.A.A. Expenses 10,000 Rds. Defensive fires at 9.2nd & 7.3. (TEMPLE UN CEMETERY) stood to & guns mounted until shelling finished down. 42035 Cpl. Thompson P. proceeds on leave to U.K. 58850 A/Cpl. Inwood D. ↑ 45368 Pte Chapters H.J. returns from leave to U.K. 37683 CSM. Rice J.A. Sous 58348 Pte Wrightson T. returns from leave to dist. 67348 Pte Downing W.B. Course. admitted to hospital.	
"	6/2/18		34301 Pte Storey proceeds on leave to U.K. 42007 Pte Tyas A. 58401 Pte Greenhalgh J. & 58562 Pte Hemingway J.S. return from leave to U.K. 122996 Pte Lucas J. evacuates to No.34 C.C.S. two struck off strength.	W.K
"	4/2/18		Sullivan 42030 Sergt Woodall R. & 38890 Pte Moran R.R. proceeds on leave to U.K. Sgt S. 57733 Cpl Clague G.G. & 38859 Pte Pollard S.J. returns from leave to U.K. Harris 58590 Pte Pitts J.H. proceed to attend a gas course at VIII Corps Gas School PERONNE	
"	8/2/18		Sullivan 81590 Pte Kerry G. proceeds on leave to U.K. 58385 A/Cpl. Inwood E. 58305 Dixon W.D. & 36440 Pte Pugh J. returns from leave to U.K.	
"	9/2/18		Lime 65543 Pte Price A.B. & 81573 Pte Masters to proceed on leave to U.K. 37349 A/Cpl Hopkinson F.F. & 67399 Pte Bacon P. returns from leave to U.K. 2nd Lieut. Pruntz 210932 proceed to 5th Army Infantry School Capt Findall for Course	

WAR DIARY
INTELLIGENCE SUMMARY

Army Form C. 2118.

Place	Date	Hour	Summary of Events and Information	Remarks and references to Appendices
POISEL	10/2/18	Fine	106040 Pte Pethard J returns from Sanitary & instructional course. 61571 Pte Patmore G proceeds on leave to UK. 57857I Pte Hudson AR 59706 Pte Gregory A 35849 L/Cpl Frost G 58604 Pte Curtis J return from leave to UK. At 4:55 pm the enemy opened an intense bombardment on our left. S.O.S. signal was sent up & artillery MG fire replied immediately All clear 5:15 pm SAA expended on & harassing fire 10,000 rds. S.O.S.	
"	11/2/18	Fine	59553 Pte Gad J Pb. proceeds on leave to UK. 58871 Pte Baugh L 36135 Pte Quinn JR return from leave to UK	
"	12/2/18	Fine	SAA expended by guns at BOBBY QUARRY on harassing fire: 5000 rds. 2/Lt AH Robinson returns from leave to UK. 82029 Pte Todd G on 10 proceeds Veterinary Course on leave to UK. 102406 L/Cpl Armstrong WA returns from Gas Course L/A Harris T 58590 Pte Pitts RA return from Gas Course.	
"	13/2/18	Rain	At 12:20 am a heavy bombardment opened out on our right & continued until 1:10 am after which time it gradually died down and stopped at 1:40 am. 10,000 rds SAA expended by barrage guns. L/Cpl Atkinson H 57931 A/Cpl Tolant J 10819 Pte Hearn J return from leave to UK. 82619 Pte Woollard J 35649 Pte Morgan J proceed on leave to UK.	
"	14/2/18	Fine	3000 rds expended in harassing fire on enemy trenches. 80922 Pte Fidwort + 35070 Pte Knight HJ proceed on leave to UK. 50774 Pte Alexander ES 35678 Pte Powers G + 57934 L/Cpl Gallivant G return from leave to UK 57932 Pte Blague GC proceeds to AVC Course.	

Army Form C. 2118.

WAR DIARY
or
INTELLIGENCE SUMMARY.
(Erase heading not required.)

Place	Date	Hour	Summary of Events and Information	Remarks and references to Appendices
ROISEL	15/2/18		10,000 rds S.A.A. expended in harassing fire on enemy trenches. 45338 Sgt Livingston & 83748 Sgt Thomas & 29930 Pte Henderson A. proceed on leave to U.K. 16/2/18. 53971 Pte Woods F. return from leave to U.K.	
	16/2/18		10,000 rds S.A.A. expended on harassing fire. 10811 Pte Tucker W. proceeds on leave to U.K. 55399 A/Cpl Bingham D & 58808 A/Cpl Brixton F. return from leave to U.K. Capt J. Green proceed on leave to U.K. 2nd Lt J.A. Hanson takes over command of Company.	
	17/2/18		5000 rds S.A.A. expended in harassing fire. 35981 Pte Sharrat W. & 58574 Pte Morton G. 103443 Pte Hardy R. proceed on leave to U.K. 39799 L/Cpl Owen Ll. 103447 Pte Thomas Aw. 104/6/8 Pte 84264 & 2nd Lt J. Duffell Z. & 55093 Pte Smith A. return from signalling course. Pte Moore J.G. 133,164	
	18/2/18		84804 A/Cpl Brackle W.A. 58573 Pte Wheaton 6 + 34710 Pte Grant G. proceed on leave to U.K. 2nd Lt J. Borden & 69343 Pte Downs J. returned from leave to U.K. 4,500 rds expended in harassing fire. returned from hospital.	
	19/2/18		4500 rds expended by guns at BOBBY QUARRY. 43178 A/Cpl Tyler G & 2nd Lt V.B. Smith Jr. 83397 Pte Dawson J. proceed on leave to U.K. 20325 58325 Pt Aldridge Jr 4357 Pte Broadhead a. returned from leave to U.K. 34765 Pte Scott A 18932 Pte Bunn P. Pte Sealey (8th Queens) returned to his battalion. A/1st R Freeland & 34679 3rd Rifle Brigade & P.A.L Daley H. 32571 Pte Brown A. 8th Queens report & are taken on strength, awaiting Pte Gummingson P. 37901 Pte Belouille J proceeds to ABBEVILLE to bring up transfer to MGC. remounts.	

WAR DIARY
or
INTELLIGENCE SUMMARY

Army Form C. 2118.

Place	Date	Hour	Summary of Events and Information	Remarks and references to Appendices
ROISEL	20/2/18	Fine	5000 rds S.A.A. expended in harassing fire. E.A. flew low over our lines at 11.0am & was engaged by our guns. The machine was seen to be hit & made a steep dive (probably enemy's lines.) 105480 Pte Shilsby & 67305 Pte Brown proceed on leave to UK. 64813 Pte Warner G. returned fr. leave to UK. 33741 L/Cpl Waring G. returned from Infantry Course. 241667 Pte Wood H. reports from 8th Bn N. Staffords & is taken on strength awaiting transfer to MGC.	
"	21/2/18	Dull & wet	4500 rds S.A.A. expended in harassing fire. 28th Div D. Jenkins Hele proceed on leave to UK. 58850 Pte Ruddy C. & 55767 Pte Hewitt H. & 126038 Pte Lynch & 125049 Pte Cottrill & 24305 Pte Robinson H. report from Base Depot & are taken on strength awaiting transfer. Pte Smith W. of 9th Bn E. Surreys report & are taken on strength. T 203325 T 203325 to MGC.	
"	22/2/18	Wet	4000 rds S.A.A. expended by barrage guns. 42035 6bd rd Thompson. Previous from leave to UK. 9930 Pte Hallows B. 10th North Staffords reports & is taken on strength awaiting transfer to MGC.	
"	23/2/18	Dull	4 guns at BEDDY QUARRY supplying right barrage relieved by #guns 17th Infantry & 4 guns supplying left barrage are withdrawn. 4 guns at TEMPLEUX CEMETERY relieved by 3 guns of 73rd M.G.Coy. 58588 Pte Bodley G. & 34301 Pte Stacey J. return from leave to UK.	
"	24/2/18	Fine	Company cleaning up after being relieved from line. 37683 L/Cpl Rice G. N.B.W. 42035 L/Cpl Thompson F (MSM) 36198 Sgt Morgan P. (Crois de Guerre) presented with respective ribbons by Army Corps Commander at MONTIGNY. L/Sgt P. Kimber & 36198 Sgt Morgan P. (19/14 Stars) addressed along with other 1914 men. 58870 Pte Moon P. & 8590 Pte Booker P. (9th R.D.Dragoons) returns from leave to UK	

Army Form C. 2118.

WAR DIARY
or
INTELLIGENCE SUMMARY.
(Erase heading not required.)

Instructions regarding War Diaries and Intelligence Summaries are contained in F.S. Regs., Part II. and the Staff Manual respectively. Title pages will be prepared in manuscript.

Place	Date	Hour	Summary of Events and Information	Remarks and references to Appendices
BOISEL	25/2/18	Fine.	237411 Cpl Robinson & 4-58588 Pte Bradley to proceed to VAIRE to arrange billets for move. 81583 Pte Masters to return from leave to U.K. 4587 Pte Bignall A. & 5 Pte Radford & 51009 Pte Dawson & 13th Middlesex report and are taken on strength awaiting transfer to mob. Company preparing to move out on rest.	
	26.2.18	Still	Transport commence march to BOVES Area. Orders received 9th in that Company will proceed to BERTEAUCOURT or THENNES as billets are not available in VAIRE. Company preparing to move 81571 Pte Paterson & 76825 Pte Price A.B. return from leave to U.K.	
BERTEAUCOURT	27.2.18	Still raw	Company move to rest in BERTEAUCOURT. 23235 Pte Doyle (8th Queen's) returns from hospital	
	28.2.18	Cold showers	Company cleaning billets & making them comfortable. Orders received at 11.45 pm that Company is to entrain at VILLERS BRETTONEUX for LA CHAPELETTE at 7 am march to DEVISE to be Cavalry Corps Reserve	

www.ingramcontent.com/pod-product-compliance
Lightning Source LLC
Chambersburg PA
CBHW081550160426
43191CB00011B/1891